BIBLE NEWS PROPHECY

 16

 19

 28

In This Issue:

2   **From the Editor: 20 Prophetic Items to Watch For in 2020** Many events will align with properly understood biblical prophecies in 2020.

16   **The Sixth Commandment** Do not kill. Is there more to this command than not murdering?

19   **Study the Bible Course Test 4.** This test is related to lessons 13 through 16 of this course.

28   **Faith** Do you know much about faith? Do you know how important faith is?

33   **How Will God Judge You?** The Bible teaches that "we shall be judged according to our works." Have you seriously considered that?

37   **Questions and Answers** How do I honor an unknown parent? Can a woman wear makeup? When is Abib? Isn't it too hard to be a Christian?

Back Cover: Internet and Radio This shows where people can find the messages from the *Continuing Church of God.*

About the Front Cover: Many say that hindsight is 20/20, but biblical prophecies help provide some 20/20 foresight. James Erwin Estoque put this together using images from sources such as Public Domain, Pixabay and Pexels.com.

Bible News Prophecy magazine is published by the Continuing Church of God, 1036 W. Grand Avenue, Grover Beach, CA, 93433. http://www.ccog.org

©2018 Continuing Church of God. Printed in the U.S.A. All rights reserved.

Reproduction in whole or in part without written permission is prohibited. We do respect your privacy and we do not rent, trade, or sell our mailing list. If you do not want to receive this magazine, simply contact our Grover Beach office. Scripture references are from the New King James Version (©Thomas Nelson, Inc., Publishers, used by permission or for 20th century articles the KJV) unless otherwise noted.

Bible News Prophecy-SUPPORTED BY YOUR CONTRIBUTIONS

Bible News Prophecy has no subscription or newsstand price. This magazine is provided free of charge by the Continuing Church of God. It is made possible by the voluntary, freely given tithes and offerings of the membership of the Church and others who have elected to support the work of the Church. Contributions are gratefully welcomed and are tax-deductible in the U.S. Those who wish to voluntarily aid and support this worldwide Work of God are gladly welcomed as co-workers in this major effort to preach and publish the gospel to all nations. Contributions should be sent to: Continuing Church of God, 1036 W. Grand Avenue, Grover Beach, CA, 93433.

Editor in Chief: Bob Thiel

Copy/Proofing Editor: Joyce Thiel

Proofreader: John Hickey; SBC Course Assister: Shirley Gestro.

Photos: All photos come from the Thiel family or public domain sources such as Wikipedia, Pixabay, or certain governments (unless specific attribution is given).

Layout and Design:
James Erwin EStoque

January - March 2020

FROM THE EDITOR IN CHIEF: BOB THIEL

20 PROPHETIC ITEMS to WATCH For in 2020

Jesus told His follower to watch (Mark 13; Luke 21). There are many events that fall under this category.

Since the sermon I gave in December 2018, titled 19 items to prophetically watch in 2018, certain world events aligned with all 19 of them. Properly understood biblical prophecies are coming to pass.

So now, let's look at 20 prophetic items to watch for further fulfilment steps in 2020.

1. Scoffers and the Modern Media

The mainstream news media seems to relish promoting then denouncing false prophecies. Many in the alternative media do that as well.

Each year, some make false prophecies related to the Great Tribulation and Jesus' return. Some expect one of both of those events in 2020. Yet, the Great Tribulation will not start then nor will Jesus return in 2020.

Sometimes, false prophecies get significant media attention.

On the other hand, properly understood biblical prophecies, like those in the process of being fulfilled get little media attention--and almost none from 'mainstream' news sources.

Why?

Well, the mainstream media (along with most academics and governmental leaders and internet posters) do not believe the Bible--and even among those who claim to, even less understand and believe biblical prophecies.

The Apostle Peter was inspired to write the following:

> 1 Beloved, I now write to you this second epistle (in both of which I stir up your pure minds by way of reminder), 2 that you may be mindful of the words which were spoken before by the holy prophets, and of the commandment of us, the apostles of the Lord and Savior, 3 knowing this first: that scoffers will come in the last days, walking according to their own lusts, 4 and saying, "Where is the promise of His coming? For since the fathers fell asleep, all things continue as they were from the beginning of creation." 5 For this they willfully forget: that by the word of God the heavens were of old, and the earth standing out of water and in the water, 6 by which the world that then existed perished, being flooded with water. 7 But the heavens and the earth which are now preserved by the same word, are reserved for fire until the day of judgment and perdition of ungodly men.
>
> 8 But, beloved, do not forget this one thing, that with the Lord one day is as a thousand years, and a thousand years as one day. 9 The Lord is not slack concerning His promise, as some count slackness, but is longsuffering toward us, not willing that any should perish but that all should come to repentance. (2 Peter 3:1-9)

There are many scoffers during these last days.

Many (mainly on the internet) have repeatedly and falsely called me a false prophet and said other bad things about me as well as the Continuing Church of God.

While that turns some away from looking at us, we understand that Jesus said this was to be expected:

> 10 Blessed are those who are persecuted for righteousness' sake, For theirs is the kingdom

of heaven. 11 Blessed are you when they revile and persecute you, and say all kinds of evil against you falsely for My sake. 12 Rejoice and be exceedingly glad, for great is your reward in heaven, for so they persecuted the prophets who were before you (Matthew 5:10-12)

We are not to turn away from true understanding of biblical prophecies, but rejoice in going through open doors to proclaim the truth while holding fast to the truth (cf. Revelation 3:7-13).

2. Morality Prophecies Being Fulfilled Daily

Some morality prophecies will be to be fulfilled daily in 2020, consistent with what the Apostle Paul wrote to the prophetic-evangelist Timothy:

> 1 But know this, that in the last days perilous times will come: 2 For men will be lovers of themselves, lovers of money, boasters, proud, blasphemers, disobedient to parents, unthankful, unholy, 3 unloving, unforgiving, slanderers, without self-control, brutal, despisers of good, 4 traitors, headstrong, haughty, lovers of pleasure rather than lovers of God, 5 having a form of godliness but denying its power. And from such people turn away! 6 For of this sort are those who creep into households and make captives of gullible women loaded down with sins, led away by various lusts, 7 always learning and never able to come to the knowledge of the truth. (2 Timothy 3:1-7)

We see this being fulfilled, not just by terrorists, but by politicians, media experts, academia, and even with scientists.

Like so-called scientists pushing aspects of evolution instead of creation (see also our free booklet, online at www.ccog.org, titled: Is God's Existence Logical?). And certain professionals who do not wish to accept biological gender.

Watch for this among leaders and the media, as well as with regular folks.

3. Internet and Other Censorship

More and more governments are putting in procedures and/or laws to restrict what is allowed on the internet. Various forms of media are doing this as well.

Furthermore then, of course, there is the LBGTQ crowd and those that promote various forms of sexual immorality. The LGBTQ crowd, as well as others who oppose aspects of biblical morality, do not want immoral behaviours labelled as sin.

Since they do not believe what the Bible says about sin, one would think that they would not care that they are considered by Christians as sinful.

Yet, they have been able to silence and/or intimidate many leaders who claim to believe the Bible as well as get laws and court decisions to support them.

Consider also the following:

> 18 For the wrath of God is revealed from heaven against all ungodliness and unrighteousness of men, who suppress the truth in unrighteousness, ... 22 Professing to be wise, they became fools, 23 and changed the glory of the incorruptible God into an image made like corruptible man — and birds and four-footed animals and creeping things.
>
> 24 Therefore God also gave them up to uncleanness, in the lusts of their hearts, to dishonor their bodies among themselves, 25 who exchanged the truth of God for the lie ...
>
> 26 For this reason God gave them up to vile passions. For even their women exchanged the natural use for what is against nature. 27 Likewise also the men, leaving the natural use of the woman, burned in their lust for one another, men with men committing what is shameful, and receiving in themselves the penalty of their error which was due.
>
> 28 And even as they did not like to retain God in their knowledge, God gave them over to a debased mind, to do those things which are not

fitting; 29 being filled with all unrighteousness, sexual immorality, wickedness, covetousness, maliciousness; full of envy, murder, strife, deceit, evil-mindedness; they are whisperers, 30 backbiters, haters of God, violent, proud, boasters, inventors of evil things, disobedient to parents, 31 undiscerning, untrustworthy, unloving, unforgiving, unmerciful; 32 who, knowing the righteous judgment of God, that those who practice such things are deserving of death, not only do the same but also approve of those who practice them. (Romans 1:18,22-25a, 26-32)

Notice that the Bible teaches that even approving of forms of sexual immorality is wrong.

The Bible also teaches:

11 "Behold, the days are coming," says the Lord God,
That I will send a famine on the land,
Not a famine of bread,
Nor a thirst for water,
But of hearing the words of the Lord.
12 They shall wander from sea to sea,
And from north to east;
They shall run to and fro, seeking the word of the Lord,
But shall not find it. (Amos 8:11-12)

That does not mean that there will be no Bibles. But the time will come when those promoting various biblical teachings will no longer to be able to have access to the internet, etc. as before. We are seeing more and more of this.

And this especially includes Europe, which has been pressuring social media companies to censor and remove 'offensive' materials.

Watch for moves to restrict rights to object to biblical sins as well as to explain certain biblical prophecies.

4. Weather Sorrows, Troubles and Earthquakes

Of course, when thinking about prophecies, most people are concerned about prophecies such as those related to world events, the beginning of sorrows, the four horsemen of the apocalypse, the Great Tribulation, the rise of the Beast/Antichrist/666, Armageddon, etc.

Jesus said:

5 And Jesus, answering them, began to say: "Take heed that no one deceives you. 6 For many will come in My name, saying, 'I am He,' and will deceive many. 7 But when you hear of wars and rumors of wars, do not be troubled; for such things must happen, but the end is not yet. 8 For nation will rise against nation, and kingdom against kingdom. And there will be earthquakes in various places, and there will be famines and troubles. These are the beginnings of sorrows. (Mark 13:5-8)

We have seen a lot of 'extreme weather' in various parts of the world in the past few years. Expect more to come:

19 Behold, a whirlwind of the Lord has gone forth in fury —
A violent whirlwind!
It will fall violently on the head of the wicked.
20 The anger of the Lord will not turn back
Until He has executed and performed the thoughts of His heart.
In the latter days you will understand it perfectly. (Jeremiah 23:19-20)

The highest all-time temperature month was recorded in July 2019. As we get closer to the end, there will be more extreme weather in places.
Jesus taught:

7 For nation will rise against nation, and kingdom against kingdom. And there will be famines, pestilences, and earthquakes in various places. (Matthew 24:7).

Expect serious earthquakes in 2020.

Though we will NOT have the earthquake of Revelation 16:18 as that happens during the Day of the Lord, that earthquake will be bigger than what the usual 'experts' have believed was possible. It will change the planet and humble parts of humanity.

But understand, that an earthquake that triggers a massive volcano, such as the USA has in places like Yellowstone and New Zealand has in places like Rotorua, can dramatically change the world. There is also Iceland and the Cascades in the USA. And without volcanos, the San Andreas, Wilimington, New Madrid, and other faults.

5. The White Horse of the Apocalypse

The Book of Revelation teaches about riders of four different coloured horses in its sixth chapter. Notice the following about the first horseman:

> 1 Now I saw when the Lamb opened one of the seals; and I heard one of the four living creatures saying with a voice like thunder, "Come and see."
>
> 2 And I looked, and behold, a white horse. He who sat on it had a bow; and a crown was given to him, and he went out conquering and to conquer. (Revelation 6:1-2)

This horseman has to do with spreading false religion. The fact that the horse is white makes the religious message being spread look like it is good.

But the Bible warns about that:

> 12 But what I do, I will also continue to do, that I may cut off the opportunity from those who desire an opportunity to be regarded just as we are in the things of which they boast. 13 For such are false apostles, deceitful workers, transforming themselves into apostles of Christ. 14 And no wonder! For Satan himself transforms himself into an angel of light. 15 Therefore it is no great thing if his ministers also transform themselves into ministers of righteousness, whose end will be according to their works. (2 Corinthians 11:12-15)

Jesus warned about false religion:

> 4 And Jesus answered and said to them: "Take heed that no one deceives you. 5 For many will come in My name, saying, 'I am the Christ,' and will deceive many. (Matthew 24:4-5)

We saw the Vatican use a 'Chrislam cross' in its outreach towards Muslims in 2019.

We are seeing the development of an interfaith, ecumenical religion which offers salvation to humanity through a humanistic climate and social agenda.

This is a false gospel. Expect more and more to accept some version of it.

6. Strife and the Red Horse of War

Notice the following:

> 3 When He opened the second seal, I heard the second living creature saying, "Come and see." 4 Another horse, fiery red, went out. And it was granted to the one who sat on it to take peace from the earth, and that people should kill one another; and there was given to him a great sword. (Revelation 6:3-4)

Somewhat paralleling the ride of the second horseman of Revelation 6:3-4, Jesus warned about wars and disturbances:

> 6 And you will hear of wars and rumors of wars. See that you are not troubled; for all these things must come to pass, but the end is not yet. 7 For nation will rise against nation, and kingdom against kingdom. (Matthew 24:6-7a)

"Nation ... against nation" is literally "ethnos ... against ethnos" in the original Greek. Notice how the Orthodox Jewish Bible translates the first half of Matthew 24:7:

> For there will be an intifada of ethnic group against ethnic group,

So, look for ethnic and racial strife in various parts of the world.

We have seen issues with Syria and the Palestinians, and more is expected one day (Isaiah 17:1). And let's not overlook Israel and Iran (cf. Isaiah 22:1-14). There are also issues between Pakistan and India as well as issues in many parts of the world. More division will one day hit the USA as well as parts of Europe.

7. Trade

Not all warfare is militaristic. There is also economic warfare.

This often involves trade.

USA tariffs, sanctions, and other 'trade war' matters were prominent in 2019. USA actions against many nations are also driving nations to look to Europe.

The Bible shows that Babylonian Europe will dominate trade (cf. Revelation 18:2-3). In 2019, we saw the Europeans making trade-related deals with the Mexicans, Japanese, and parts of South America (the South American Mercosur deal was the biggest trade deal ever by the EU). We also saw them, as well as other nations, upset with the USA and various aspects of its trade and tariff policies.

Look for Europe to work to make more trade deals.

Expect more trade issues in 2020.

8. The Deal of Daniel 9:27

In 2019, parts of the Trump Administration's 'deal of the century' were revealed. The reactions by the Palestinians have mainly been negative.

Despite Palestinian angst, a deal will happen.

The Bible teaches that a deal will be confirmed for a seven-year period by a European leader who will later rise up and stop animal sacrifices at the mid-point:

> 26 And the people of the prince who is to come
> Shall destroy the city and the sanctuary.
> The end of it shall be with a flood,
> And till the end of the war desolations are determined.
> 27 Then he shall confirm a covenant with many for one week;
> But in the middle of the week
> He shall bring an end to sacrifice and offering.
> And on the wing of abominations shall be one who makes desolate,
> Even until the consummation, which is determined,
> Is poured out on the desolate (Daniel 9:26-27).

The 'one week' time element has generally been understood by prophecy watchers to mean a seven year deal (2520 days, based on prophetic 360 day years), that will be broken in the middle of it (after 3 1/2 years). The Hebrew word translated as 'week' literally means 'sevened' (OT:7620 literal, sevened. Biblesoft's New Exhaustive Strong's Numbers and Concordance with Expanded Greek-Hebrew Dictionary. © 2006).

While Daniel 9:26 calls the leader who confirms the deal a 'prince', he is later is referred to as the king of the dominating European empire (Daniel 11:40).

One way to show this is a European empire is to realize that it was the people of the Roman Empire of the 1st century that fulfilled the portion of Daniel 9:26 as they destroyed the city (Jerusalem) in 70 A.D.

Jewish sources, while not understanding all of this, also agree that it was Roman forces that destroyed the city and sanctuary as the following demonstrates:

> "The people of the prince will come and destroy the city and the Sanctuary" Daniel 9:26, refers to the Roman legions of Vespasian and Titus, who destroyed Jerusalem. (Daniel 9 – A True Biblical Interpretation. Jews for Judaism. Accessed 07/30/16)

In the 21st century, the European Union includes much of the land and peoples that were part of the ancient Roman Empire. And it is the 'prince' coming from that people that verse 27 of Daniel 9 is referring to. Thus, this prophecy tells us that a lower level European leader will somewhat officially start to rise up about 3 ½ years before the great tribulation (and yes, according to Jesus in Matthew 24:9, some 'tribulation' does happen prior to the start of the Great Tribulation).

Because of statements and actions by US President Donald Trump, Europeans are even more interested in being part of a Middle East peace deal.

Expect to see, at least some, European efforts along those lines. Especially if we see a major conflict in that region.

Now, once the deal is confirmed for one prophetic week (which could happen sometime AFTER a deal is made) by the 'prince', the seven-year countdown for the return of Jesus and the 3 ½ year countdown for the Great Tribulation (Matthew 24:21) will begin.

9. Knowledge Increasing

Notice something from ancient times:

> 6 And the LORD said, "Indeed the people are one and they all have one language, and this is what they begin to do; now nothing that they propose to do will be withheld from them. 7 Come, let Us go down and there confuse their language, that they may not understand one another's speech."
>
> 8 So the LORD scattered them abroad from there over the face of all the earth, and they ceased building the city. 9 Therefore its name is called Babel, because there the Lord confused the language of all the earth; and from there the Lord scattered them abroad over the face of all the earth. (Genesis 11:6-9)

While many languages came out of this, notice another prophecy for the end times:

> 4 "But you, Daniel, shut up the words, and seal the book until the time of the end; many shall run to and fro, and knowledge shall increase." (Daniel 12:4)

We are seeing massive developments in health, robotics, and various sciences.

The arrival and use of 'artificial intelligence', automobiles, jet planes, computers, and the internet certainly align with that prophecy.

Computers have also made it easier to communicate, even among people of different languages.

Those who do not accept biblical prophecy seem to consider the knowledge explosion and ability to travel internationally irrelevant.

Yet, those of us who believe it consider this a confirmed prophecy. And this is a prophecy of around 2600 years old!

Expect to see more knowledge developments.

10. Debt

The Bible teaches that the result of debt accumulation will be far worse than even many pessimists believe.

Notice the first part of an end-time prophecy given to the prophet Habakkuk by God over 2600 years ago:

> 2 And the Lord answered me:
> "Write the vision; make it plain on tablets,
> so he may run who reads it.
> 3 For still the vision awaits its appointed time;
> it hastens to the end—it will not lie.
> If it seems slow, wait for it;
> it will surely come; it will not delay. (Habakkuk 2:2-3, English Standard Version)

So, this prophecy is so bad that God says people need to take action.

However, many are too puffed up, too arrogant to consider that it will really happen in the 21st century:

> 4 "Behold, his soul is puffed up; it is not upright within him,
> but the righteous shall live by his faith.
> 5 "Moreover, wine is a traitor,
> an arrogant man who is never at rest.
> His greed is as wide as Sheol;
> like death he has never enough.
> He gathers for himself all nations
> and collects as his own all peoples." (Habakkuk 2:4-5, ESV)

So, a puffed up, arrogant, and greedy people are involved.

This is a people that is heavily indebted:

> 6 Shall not all these take up their taunt against him, with scoffing and riddles for him, and say, "Woe to him who heaps up what is not his own—for how long?—and loads himself with pledges!" (Habakkuk 2:6, ESV)

Treasury bills are a form of pledges that the USA has continued to heap up. The USA is the most indebted nation in the history of humanity and those in it should try to understand this prophecy. In 2019 its government officials made a deal to increase the debt level in 2020. More debt will hit the USA and debt will be a factor in its destruction.

(Perhaps it should be noted that both the United Kingdom and Canada have very high per capita debt levels.)

Notice what will happen:

> 7 Will not your debtors suddenly arise, and those awake who will make you tremble? Then you will be spoil for them. (Habakkuk 2:7, ESV)

When it is time, destruction will be sudden!

Why?

> 8 Because you have plundered many nations, all the remnant of the peoples shall plunder you, for the blood of man and violence to the earth, to cities and all who dwell in them. (Habakkuk 2:8; ESV)

The USA has plundered many nations by borrowing and importing without the intention to truly pay back.

The USA has had violent bloody interventions around the world.

Should interest rates ever rise to historical levels, this will cause massive financial problems for the USA.

When foreigners finally have had enough, it will not end well for the USA.

God told Habakkuk that this should be a very serious matter.

Have you been paying attention to this?

II. US Dollar Dominance will Decrease

Consider the following curse from the Book of Leviticus:

> 19 I will break the pride of your power; (Leviticus 26:19)

While the above undoubtedly has military & economic possibilities, consider that the US dollar is the pride of the USA's power.

It is backed by nothing.

So, it is a prideful thing--plus it does project US power around the world.

Debt, trade, weather, morality, leadership, sanctions, and other issues have given various nations motivations to work to dethrone the US dollar as the world's primary trade and reserve currency.

The economy of the USA has been financed, to a significant degree, by foreigners willing to provide goods to the USA on credit as well as the USA profiting from much of the rest of the world's international trade that is dollar-based.

Yet, because of recent US actions which many believe have 'weaponized' its dollar, more nations are looking for ways to bypass the US dollar in trade. The EU, for example, came up with its Instex system to bypass the US dominated SWIFT system for processing international transactions.

The time will come when the US dollar is dethroned and this will inflict great pain on the USA. But near the time the US dollar becomes close to worthless, the great tribulation (Matthew 24:21) will come and the USA will then be no more. The Europeans, BRICS's (Brazil, Russia, China, India, South Africa) nations, Iran, Venezuela, Turkey, North Korea, and others want to dethrone the USA dollar.

Dethroning the US dollar will cause massive economic problems for the USA. Much more than almost anyone believes. The standard of living in the USA has been raised/subsidized for years because of the status of the US dollar.

That status is weakening. This will ultimately severely hurt the USA.

12. Cash and 666

Notice the following prophecy:

> 16 He causes all, both small and great, rich and poor, free and slave, to receive a mark on their right hand or on their foreheads, 17 and that no one may buy or sell except one who has the mark or the name of the beast, or the number of his name.
>
> 18 Here is wisdom. Let him who has understanding calculate the number of the beast, for it is the number of a man: His number is 666. (Revelation 13:16-18)

It will be a European power that will truly fulfill the above prophecy of 666. In 2019, the EU announced that it was intending setting up an enforcer of financial matters that should be begin in 2020 or 2021. Europe will need to have some type of enforcer for Revelation 13:16-17 to be fulfilled—and it is intending to have one.

It will likely take computers aided with artificial intelligence to aid in the fulfillment of the scriptures in Revelation 13:15-18, as well as cyber-spying/monitoring.

This type of financial surveillance could not have happened during the time of the Apostle John as there was no real way to monitor many financial transactions then. The same was true for all the centuries that followed until the late 20th and now the 21st century. But now not only does the technology exist to monitor most financial transactions, the political will is there as well.

While 2020 will not see a completely cashless world, expect to see more movements towards monitorable payments.

13. Gold

The fall of the US dollar and the trend towards digital money will concern many.

While some economists have called gold a 'relic', it still has value internationally.

The old Worldwide Church of God published the following:

> Of course, since gold is regarded as a disaster hedge by many investors, prudence might dictate that perhaps a small fraction of your liquid assets be in gold: (Caulkins J. WHEN MONEY FAILS. Good News, October-November 1979)
>
> In Revelation 18, we are given a graphic description of Europe at its future economic peak. Remember this prophecy occurs after the United States, Canada and other Israelitish nations have been conquered and brought into subservience. ...
>
> In verse 11, Europe's coming economic wealth and scope is described as John sees it, shortly before the final crisis (to occur at Christ's coming) takes place.
>
> "And the merchants of the earth shall weep and mourn over her, for no man buyeth their merchandise any more: The merchandise of gold and silver ... (Catherwood CA. Europe and Our Prophetic Message. Good News, October-November 1979)

Yes, gold will outlast the US dollar and the European Beast power will have it.

The Bible prophesies that the King of the North will get gold which end time Babylon will also trade with:

> 37 He shall regard neither the God of his fathers nor the desire of women, nor regard any god; for he shall exalt himself above them all. 38 But in their place he shall honor a god of fortresses; and a god which his fathers did not know he shall honor with gold and silver, with precious stones and pleasant things. 39 Thus he shall act

against the strongest fortresses with a foreign god, which he shall acknowledge, and advance its glory; and he shall cause them to rule over many, and divide the land for gain. 40 "At the time of the end the king of the South shall attack him; and the king of the North shall come against him like a whirlwind, ... 43 He shall have power over the treasures of gold and silver, and over all the precious things of Egypt ... (Daniel 11:37-40,43)

10 ... 'Alas, alas, that great city Babylon, that mighty city! For in one hour your judgment has come.' 11 And the merchants of the earth will weep and mourn over her, for no one buys their merchandise anymore: 12 merchandise of gold and silver, precious stones and pearls, fine linen and purple, silk and scarlet, every kind of citron wood, every kind of object of ivory, every kind of object of most precious wood, bronze, iron, and marble; ... 15 The merchants of these things, who became rich by her, will stand at a distance for fear of her torment, weeping and wailing, 16 and saying, 'Alas, alas, that great city that was clothed in fine linen, purple, and scarlet, and adorned with gold and precious stones and pearls! (Revelation 18:10-12,15-16)

While the Bible is clear that gold will, for a time, not be wanted but tossed (Ezekiel 7:19)—hence it will be worse than useless for a time—it obvious that into the beginning years of the Great Tribulation (Matthew 24:21-22), which starts in verse 39 of Daniel 11, gold will have value.

Now, understand that Germany has been repatriating gold--and even did so ahead of schedule. Other European nations such as the Netherlands, Austria, Poland, Belgium, and Hungary have been or are in the process of repatriating gold and/or increasing their gold reserves as well.

Furthermore, Russia and China have greatly increasing their gold reserves.

Russia, Turkey, and China have been looking to use gold for trade to bypass the USA dollar.

While the price of gold will likely have ups and downs in 2020, gold will have value after the USA dollar does not.

14. Europe Will Work to Reorganize

The Bible shows that Europe will have problems with truly being united:

> 41 Whereas you saw the feet and toes, partly of potter's clay and partly of iron, the kingdom shall be divided; yet the strength of the iron shall be in it, just as you saw the iron mixed with ceramic clay. 42 And as the toes of the feet were partly of iron and partly of clay, so the kingdom shall be partly strong and partly fragile. 43 As you saw iron mixed with ceramic clay, they will mingle with the seed of men; but they will not adhere to one another, just as iron does not mix with clay. (Daniel 2:41-43)

Expect to see problems, as well as opportunities, with European unity in 2020.

Despite problems, the Bible also shows that Europe will reorganize:

> 12 The ten horns which you saw are ten kings who have received no kingdom as yet, but they receive authority for one hour as kings with the beast. 13 These are of one mind, and they will give their power and authority to the beast. (Revelation 17:12-13).

Various ones are calling for a version of that in Europe. Even Pope Francis has called for Europe to be creative and think beyond national boundaries.

Back in 2011, Ursula von der Leyen (who was elected as the new EU Commission President in 2019) said: "My aim is a united states of Europe."

The idea of a United States of Europe has been something that Church of God leaders have written about for decades. United Europe will appear for a time, even though Ursula von der Leyen backed off her statement in 2019.

The prophesied reorganizations in Revelation 17:12-13

will not happen in 2020, but expect calls to reorganize Europe and improve European unity.

15. Europe Will Develop its Military

The Bible shows that Europe will become a major military power:

> 24 He shall enter peaceably, even into the richest places of the province; and he shall do what his fathers have not done, nor his forefathers: he shall disperse among them the plunder, spoil, and riches; and he shall devise his plans against the strongholds, but only for a time. 25 He shall stir up his power and his courage against the king of the South with a great army. (Daniel 11:24-25)

Notice that the 'he', which is a European power, will first seem peaceful, but will end up having a great army!

Europe is working on developing its own army. It even has an umbrella structure called PESCO (PErmanent Structured COoperation). Nearly all the EU nations are officially part of PESCO. The plan is to develop military technology and a unified European military.

One that is independent of the USA.

Furthermore, Europe has been working on technology, like the Large Hadron Collider and its Galileo satellite system, in order to give it capabilities independent of the USA.

Europe has been getting its Galileo satellites launched and expects to be fully operational in 2020.

This is a trend to watch. Germany will take steps to promote a stronger military.

While most do not believe that Europe can or ever will destroy the USA, consider the following prophecies:

> 5 "Woe to Assyria, the rod of My anger And the staff in whose hand is My indignation. 6 I will send him against an ungodly nation, And against the people of My wrath I will give him charge, To seize the spoil, to take the prey, And to tread them down like the mire of the streets. 7 Yet he does not mean so, Nor does his heart think so; But it is in his heart to destroy, And cut off not a few nations. ... 11 As I have done to Samaria and her idols, Shall I not do also to Jerusalem and her idols?' 12 Therefore it shall come to pass, when the Lord has performed all His work on Mount Zion and on Jerusalem, that He will say, "I will punish the fruit of the arrogant heart of the king of Assyria, and the glory of his haughty looks."(Isaiah 10:5-7,11-12).

> 39 Thus he shall act against the strongest fortresses with a foreign god, which he shall acknowledge, and advance its glory; and he shall cause them to rule over many, and divide the land for gain. (Daniel 11:39)

In Isaiah 10, the reference to 'Assyria' is pointing to a German-dominated European power in the 21st century. The reference to 'Samaria' is pointing to the USA in the 21st century.

Related to Daniel 11:39, consider that in the 21st century, it is the USA with the strongest fortresses. The power with the strongest fortresses will be taken over by the European Beast power. Technology, as well as deception, will be factors in the military takeover of the USA.

This will cause the world to marvel:

> 3 And I saw one of his heads as if it had been mortally wounded, and his deadly wound was healed. And all the world marveled and followed the beast. 4 So they worshiped the dragon who gave authority to the beast; and they worshiped the beast, saying, "Who is like the beast? Who is able to make war with him?" (Revelation 13:3-4)

People will be shocked when Europe shows it is a militarily successful power. It is now taking steps that will lead to the fulfillment of various warring prophecies.

But it is too soon for the USA to be taken over in 2020. There are still other events (like the confirmation of the deal of Daniel 9:27) that still must take place first (cf. Matthew 24:4-16).

With Europeans concerned about the USA and NATO, expect more steps by the EU to develop a powerful military. Ursula von der Leyen has also called for that.

16. Steps Towards the Formation of the King of the South Will Occur

The formation of the King of the South is something to look out for.

Psalm 83 prophesies a confederacy:

> 3 They have taken crafty counsel against Your people,
> And consulted together against Your sheltered ones.
> 4 They have said, "Come, and let us cut them off from being a nation,
> That the name of Israel may be remembered no more."
> 5 For they have consulted together with one consent;
> They form a confederacy against You:
> 6 The tents of Edom and the Ishmaelites;
> Moab and the Hagrites;
> 7 Gebal, Ammon, and Amalek;
> Philistia with the inhabitants of Tyre;
> 8 Assyria also has joined with them;
> They have helped the children of Lot. (Psalm 83:3-8)

Most of the peoples listed above are currently in the Middle East and North Africa, with the exception of Assyria--which is mainly in Europe.

Notice that a deal in alluded in Daniel 11 and will be broken:

> 15 ... the king of the North ... 25 ... the king of the South ... 27 Both these kings' hearts shall be bent on evil, and they shall speak lies at the same table; but it shall not prosper, for the end will still be at the appointed time. (Daniel 11:15,25,27)

So, these powers will have make lying deals.

After the USA is taken over (Daniel 11:39), they will then turn on each other:

> 40 "At the time of the end the king of the South shall attack him; and the king of the North shall come against him like a whirlwind, with chariots, horsemen, and with many ships; and he shall enter the countries, overwhelm them, and pass through. 41 He shall also enter the Glorious Land, and many countries shall be overthrown; but these shall escape from his hand: Edom, Moab, and the prominent people of Ammon. 42 He shall stretch out his hand against the countries, and the land of Egypt shall not escape. 43 He shall have power over the treasures of gold and silver, and over all the precious things of Egypt; also the Libyans and Ethiopians shall follow at his heels. (Daniel 11:40-43)

US and European politicians have called for a confederation or coalition of nations in the Middle East and North Africa to suppress terrorism as well as deal with migrant issues.

Saudi Arabia, Egypt, and others have taken steps that will help the ultimate formation of the King of the South. There now is a military alliance among most Muslim nations in the Middle East and North Africa. There has even been a call from the USA for Middle East-North Africa 'Arab NATO'. The Bible tells of a coming confederacy coming to those lands.

While the confederacy is not expected be fully formed in 2020, watch for events that will point in its direction. A King of the South will arise, be involved in some deals, later do damage, and later be destroyed (see also Ezekiel 30:1-8).

17. The Time of the Gentiles will Lead to Armageddon

The New Testament teaches:

> 24 ... Jerusalem will be trampled by Gentiles until the times of the Gentiles are fulfilled. (Luke 21:24)

> 2 But leave out the court which is outside the temple, and do not measure it, for it has been

given to the Gentiles. And they will tread the holy city underfoot for forty-two months. (Revelation 11:2)

More Gentile-dominated groups and projects are appearing to get the world to move away from an Anglo-American dominated world order. Basically, part of the objective of the BRICS, EAEU (Eurasian Economic Union), Shanghai Cooperation Organization, and even the European Union is to establish a new world order—one no longer dominated by the USA and its Anglo-Saxon allies, like the UK.

Some few years after that new order is in place in Europe, Eurasian powers will take military steps against it:

> 16 Now the number of the army of the horsemen was two hundred million; I heard the number of them. 17 And thus I saw the horses in the vision: those who sat on them had breastplates of fiery red, hyacinth blue, and sulfur yellow; and the heads of the horses were like the heads of lions; and out of their mouths came fire, smoke, and brimstone. (Revelation 9:16-17)

> 13 And I saw three unclean spirits like frogs coming out of the mouth of the dragon, out of the mouth of the beast, and out of the mouth of the false prophet. 14 For they are spirits of demons, performing signs, which go out to the kings of the earth and of the whole world, to gather them to the battle of that great day of God Almighty. 15 "Behold, I am coming as a thief. Blessed is he who watches, and keeps his garments, lest he walk naked and they see his shame." 16 And they gathered them together to the place called in Hebrew, Armageddon. (Revelation 16:13-16).

It is only a force which includes significant involvement with Asia that could put together an army so massive in the 21st century. Actually, when the above was written in the 1st century, there were not even believed to be that many males on planet Earth. But there are clearly enough now.

Consider, further, that with its One Belt, One Road (AKA Silk Road) project, China is working on making roads that will transport troops to Armageddon. China has over 60 nations involved and, on an inflation-adjusted basis, is expected to pour ten times the amount of money into this than the USA did for its Marshall Plan, which mainly helped 6 European nations.

The gathering of Armageddon will not happen in 2020, but some events to make that gathering happen will.

18. Jews Ready to Sacrifice

The Bible teaches the following:

> 27 Then he shall confirm a covenant with many for one week;
> But in the middle of the week
> He shall bring an end to sacrifice and offering.
> And on the wing of abominations shall be one who makes desolate,
> Even until the consummation, which is determined,
> Is poured out on the desolate (Daniel 9:27).

> 31 And forces shall be mustered by him, and they shall defile the sanctuary fortress; then they shall take away the daily sacrifices, and place there the abomination of desolation. (Daniel 11:31)

Now, in order for the sacrifices to stop, they must start.

Essentially, since the destruction of Jerusalem and what is called the Second Temple in A.D. 70, the Jews stopped sacrificing animals.

Some claim that this will require what is called a Third Temple in Jerusalem. Because of Donald Trump's decision on December 6, 2017 related to recognizing Jerusalem as Israel's capital and the move of the US Embassy to Jerusalem in 2018, some think this will make it easier for a 'Third Temple' to be built there.

Some have claimed that Donald Trump is a new Cyrus. But unlike Cyrus (Isaiah 44:24-28, 45:1-4), Donald Trump was not prophesied by name to get a Jewish temple rebuilt.

Nor is a massive Third Temple in Jerusalem needed for animal sacrifices to resume. Right now, all the Jews are waiting on is for official government permission.

Biblically, they do NOT need a rebuilt Temple to sacrifice. They only need an altar, a qualified priest, and implements.

Groups like the Temple Institute and Reconstituted Sanhedrin claim to have all of that.

Notice that the Bible recorded the following:

> 6 From the first day of the seventh month began they to offer burnt offerings unto the LORD. But the foundation of the temple of the LORD was not yet laid. (Ezra 3:6)

One may argue that since it takes the participation of Jewish religious leaders in order for Jewish animal sacrifices to be resumed, that the above scripture is a moot point.

As it turns out, representatives of both the Sanhedrin and the Temple Institute have told me that they only need government permission to sacrifice, as they are basically otherwise prepared.

They did a trial sacrifice to cleanse a new altar on December 10, 2018.

So, despite what may happen in Jerusalem with the area called the Temple Mount, the Jews will one day reinstitute animal sacrifices and they do not need a Third Temple to do that.

19. The Fulfillment of Matthew 28:19-20 and Matthew 24:14

Jesus taught:

> 19 Go therefore and make disciples of all the nations, baptizing them in the name of the Father and of the Son and of the Holy Spirit, 20 teaching them to observe all things that I have commanded you; and lo, I am with you always, even to the end of the age. (Matthew 28:19-20)

In the Continuing Church of God sermons, I have gone over everything that the Bible records that Jesus spoke in the New Testament.

Additionally, this is something I instructed our ministers in Africa and Europe to do while visiting them in Nairobi, Kenya in February 2017.

We also have made literature available, not only on the internet, but in printed form and in multiple languages.

Jesus also taught:

> 14 And this gospel of the kingdom will be preached in all the world as a witness to all the nations, and then the end will come. 15 "Therefore when you see the 'abomination of desolation,' spoken of by Daniel the prophet, standing in the holy place" (whoever reads, let him understand), 16 then let those who are in Judea flee to the mountains. 17 Let him who is on the housetop not go down to take anything out of his house. 18 And let him who is in the field not go back to get his clothes. 19 But woe to those who are pregnant and to those who are nursing babies in those days! 20 And pray that your flight may not be in winter or on the Sabbath. 21 For then there will be great tribulation, such as has not been since the beginning of the world until this time, no, nor ever shall be. 22 And unless those days were shortened, no flesh would be saved; but for the elect's sake those days will be shortened. (Matthew 24:14-22)

Notice that the Great Tribulation happens after Matthew 24:14 has been fulfilled to God's satisfaction.

In the Continuing Church of God, we have a booklet, The Gospel of the Kingdom of God, available in close to 100 languages. They can be found at www.ccog.org.

The late artist Andy Warhol was known for getting the idea out that people are entitled to their 'fifteen minutes of fame'.

The Apostle Paul wrote that God would have a short

work:

> 28 For He will finish the work and cut it short in righteousness, Because the Lord will make a short work upon the earth. (Romans 9:28)

In the Continuing Church of God, we are preparing for this through the development of articles and booklets, and in numerous languages.

We believe that when we publicly identify the coming King of the North and explain that he is pushing a false peace and false gospel, and that he will destroy the USA and its Anglo-Saxon dominated allies, as well as an Islamic power, that media attention will be focused on us and what we teach.

This will be the short work, and will lead to the fulfillment of Matthew 24:14.

Are you going to watch or support the work?

Jesus praised the Philadelphians for their work (Revelation 3:7-13), while condemning the Laodicean Christians for being lukewarm about the work (Revelation 3:14-22).

But when will the end come?

When God determines that Matthew 24:14 has been fulfilled, and we of the Continuing Church of God continue to diligently work on this.

20. The US Presidential Election

The USA intends to hold a presidential election in 2020. By virtue of US influence and timing, whoever wins will be apocalyptic, meaning that he or she will (intentionally and/or inadvertently) take steps that will lead to the start of the Great Tribulation and the end of the USA.

The result of the next election will be a leader consistent with immorality prophecies such as 2 Timothy 3:1-9. Pray for God's kingdom to come (Matthew 6:10).

Summary

Many events we have seen in the 21st century align with a proper understanding of Bible prophecy. Notice what Jesus said:

> 33 Take heed, watch and pray; for you do not know when the time is. 34 It is like a man going to a far country, who left his house and gave authority to his servants, and to each his work, and commanded the doorkeeper to watch. 35 Watch therefore, for you do not know when the master of the house is coming — in the evening, at midnight, at the crowing of the rooster, or in the morning — 36 lest, coming suddenly, he find you sleeping. 37 And what I say to you, I say to all: Watch! (Mark 13:33-37)

This article has given you at least 20 things to watch for in 2020.

FREE *Continuing Church of God* Books and Booklets
at www.ccog.org/books

Christians: AMBASSADORS

Continuing History of the Church of God

Dating: A Key to Success in Marriage

Faith for Those God has Called and Chosen

The SIXTH Commandment

By Bob Thiel

Imagine a world that is safe.

Around $2 trillion dollars per year is spent on militaries worldwide. Massive amounts are also spent on police forces and security services.

Money that goes towards killing or preventing getting killed could go to aid humankind instead of protect against it.

The first physical murder recorded in the Bible is when Cain killed his brother Abel (Genesis 4:8).

But murder began before there were human beings. Notice what Jesus said:

> 44 You are of your father the devil, and the desires of your father you want to do. He was a murderer from the beginning, and does not stand in the truth, because there is no truth in him. When he speaks a lie, he speaks from his own resources, for he is a liar and the father of it. (John 8:44)

Satan's deceit to Adam and Eve ultimately resulted in their death (cf. Genesis 2:17; 5:5).

The sixth commandment, from the Book of Exodus, states:

> 13 "You shall not murder. (Exodus 20:13)

Yet, most who profess Christianity have reasoned around the truth that command contains.

Military Service and Sports

It is well documented that early Christians would not voluntarily enter the military. Nor would they watch violent sports.

Even most Greco-Romans who professed Christ held to that view until the 4th century, when most accepted the decrees and influence of the follower of the sun-god Mithras, named Constantine.

"Mithraism was first and foremost a military cult" (Aiken CF. Mithraism. The Catholic University bulletin, Volume 19, 1913, p. 255). Emperor Constantine attempted to blend his pagan views with what he considered to be Christianity (Herbermann C, Georg G. Constantine the Great. The Catholic Encyclopedia, 1908).

Many went along with Emperor Constantine.

Even Protestant reformers, including Martin Luther, took militaristic views of Christianity (cf. Luther's Works, vol. Xx, pp. 2230-2632).

Yet, Jesus taught His servants would not fight in this age (John 18:36). in His Sermon on the Mount, He taught to be angry against one without cause risked judgment (Matthew 5:22). Because of these teachings and the teaching to "love your neighbor as yourself" (Matthew 22:39), early Christians would not only not join the military, they would not even watch violent sports (cf. Theophilus of Antioch. To Autolycus, Book III, Chapter XV).

Wanting someone to be injured or to somehow be intentionally struck by someone else for entertainment does not show 'Philadelphian love' and should not be encouraged.

Philadelphia means 'brotherly love.' Yet, most who profess Christ do not seem to be bothered by encouraging violence against others.

In the Kingdom of God, "Nation shall not lift up sword against nation, Neither shall they learn war anymore" (Micah 4:3).

Control Your Anger

Jesus warned against improper anger (Matthew 5:22).

Yet some are proud of their tempers. Others blame their anger on their upbringing and/or ethnic origin and are unwilling to change. Although all are affected by their environments, we are not to nurse our anger.

But the Bible says that anger is not to control us in both the Old and New Testaments:

> 4 Be angry, and do not sin. Meditate within your heart on your bed, and be still. (Psalm 4:4)

> 32 He who is slow to anger is better than the mighty, And he who rules his spirit than he who takes a city. (Proverbs 16:32)

> 11 The discretion of a man makes him slow to anger, And his glory is to overlook a transgression. (Proverbs 19:11)

> 9 Do not hasten in your spirit to be angry, For anger rests in the bosom of fools. (Ecclesiastes 7:9)

> 26 "Be angry, and do not sin": do not let the sun go down on your wrath, 27 nor give place to the devil. (Ephesians 4:26-27)

Additionally, notice the following:

> 1 A soft answer turns away wrath, But a harsh word stirs up anger. 2 The tongue of the wise uses knowledge rightly, But the mouth of fools pours forth foolishness. (Proverbs 15:1-2)

> 18 A wrathful man stirs up strife, But he who is slow to anger allays contention. (Proverbs 15:18)

> 16 "Behold, I send you out as sheep in the midst of wolves. Therefore be wise as serpents and harmless as doves. (Matthew 10:16)

Not only are we not to be improperly angry, it is wise for God's people to help others who may be angry towards us if we can.

We are also to pray for them:

> 44 But I say to you, love your enemies, bless those who curse you, do good to those who hate you, and pray for those who spitefully use you and persecute you, 45 that you may be sons of your Father in heaven; for He makes His sun rise on the evil and on the good, and sends rain on the just and on the unjust. 46 For if you love those who love you, what reward have you? Do not even the tax collectors do the same? 47 And if you greet your brethren only, what do you do more than others? Do not even the tax collectors do so? 48 Therefore you shall be perfect, just as your Father in heaven is perfect. (Matthew 5:44-48)

Jesus set a standard above merely not murdering. We are to love and pray for our enemies and strive for perfection!

Sixth Commandment Before Sinai, from Jesus, and After Jesus' Death

The Bible shows the sixth commandment was in place before Mt. Sinai:

> "You are of your father the devil, and the desires of your father you want to do. He was a murderer from the beginning" (John 8:44) (since the devil was a murderer from the beginning it seems clear that murder was not allowed before Mount Sinai). "Cain rose up against Abel his brother and killed him…And He said, 'The voice of your brother's blood cries out to Me from the ground. So now you are cursed from the earth" (Genesis 4:8,11). "Then the king of Egypt spoke … 'When you do the duties of a midwife for the Hebrew women, and see them on the birthstools, if it is a son, then you shall kill him'…But the midwives feared God, and did not do as the king of Egypt commanded them"

(Exodus 1:15-17). "The murderer rises with the light; He kills the poor and needy" (Job 24:14).

Jesus taught and expanded the sixth commandment:

"You have heard that it was said to those of old, 'You shall not murder', and whoever murders will be in danger of the judgment. But I say to you that whoever is angry with his brother without a cause shall be in danger of the judgment" (Matthew 5:21-22). "For out of the heart proceed evil thoughts, murders…These are the things which defile a man" (Matthew 15:19-20). "You shall not murder" (Matthew 19:18). "…murders…All these evil things come from within and defile a man" (Mark 7:21,23). "Do not murder" (Mark 10:19). "You know the commandments:…Do not murder" (Luke 18:20).

Even being angry at one improperly is considered by God to be murder.

After Jesus was resurrected, the New Testament taught the sixth commandment:

"being filled with all unrighteousness…murder" (Romans 1:29). "You shall not murder" (Romans 13:9). "Now the works of the flesh are evident… murders" (Galatians 5:19,21). "the lawless and insubordinate … murders … manslayers" (1 Timothy 1:9). "But let none of you suffer as a murderer" (1 Peter 4:15). "For He who said, 'Do not commit adultery,' also said, 'Do not murder'. Now if you do not commit adultery, but you do murder, you have become a transgressor of the law" (James 2:11). "You lust…You murder" (James 4:2)."Whoever hates his brother is a murderer, and we know that no murderer has eternal life abiding in him" (1 John 3:15). "And they did not repent of their murders" (Revelation 9:21). "he who kills with the sword must be killed with the sword" (Revelation 13:10). "But …murderers… shall have their part in the lake that burns with fire and brimstone, which is the second death" (Revelation 21:8). "But outside are…murderers" (Revelation 22:15).

Notice that unrepentant murderers will not make it. They will not have access to the tree of life (Revelation 22:14).

Murderers Will Be No More

Now, consider the following:

3 And I heard a loud voice from heaven saying, "Behold, the tabernacle of God is with men, and He will dwell with them, and they shall be His people. God Himself will be with them and be their God. 4 And God will wipe away every tear from their eyes; there shall be no more death, nor sorrow, nor crying. There shall be no more pain, for the former things have passed away."

5 Then He who sat on the throne said, "Behold, I make all things new." And He said to me, "Write, for these words are true and faithful."

6 And He said to me, "It is done! I am the Alpha and the Omega, the Beginning and the End. I will give of the fountain of the water of life freely to him who thirsts. 7 He who overcomes shall inherit all things, and I will be his God and he shall be My son. 8 But the cowardly, unbelieving, abominable, murderers, sexually immoral, sorcerers, idolaters, and all liars shall have their part in the lake which burns with fire and brimstone, which is the second death." (Revelation 21:3-8)

The time is coming when there will be no more murderers. Peace will reign.

All Christians should look forward to that time.

More on the Ten Commandments can be found in our free online book, available at www.ccog.org, titled: 'The Ten Commandments: The Decalogue, Christianity, and the Beast.'

STUDY THE BIBLE COURSE

TEST 4

Bob Thiel, Editor-in-Chief
Published 2020 by the Continuing Church of God

> Preface: This course is highly based upon the personal correspondence course developed in 1954 that began under the direction of the late C. Paul Meredith in the old Radio Church of God. Various portions have been updated for the 21st century (though much of the original writing has been retained). It also has more scriptural references, as well as information and questions not in the original course. Unless otherwise noted, scriptural references are to the NKJV, copyright Thomas Nelson Publishing, used by permission. The KJV, sometimes referred to as the Authorized Version is also often used. Additionally, Catholic-approved translations such as the New Jerusalem Bible (NJB) are sometimes used as are other translations.

Test 4

This examination is given to help you better *understand* your Bible. It is related to lessons 13 through 16 of this course.

Note that there are 81 questions and that they are numbered consecutively **1, 2, 3** etc. Note also that there are *four* possible answers given under each question. These are labeled **A, B, C, D.** *ONLY ONE of these four possible answers is considered to be the RIGHT one!* —the other three are false unless stated otherwise.

YOU ARE TO SELECT THE ONE RIGHT ANSWER FROM AMONG THESE FOUR POSSIBLE ANSWERS.

You are to repeat this process for each of the questions asked. This comprises your test. (Generally speaking, the incorrect answers are false ideas which are taught and believed about the subject.)

Our objective is to give all who have determination to know God's Word the opportunity to understand the true meaning of the Bible.

By the answers you give to our examination questions, you help show if you have the desire to learn and are doing your best. We are here to aid just such people and we are thrilled to do so.

The final judge as to whether you know your Bible and are living by it will be God Himself. He is the One you had better seek to please. It is He who is able to give you eternal life.

Your eagerness to study and to make the most of your opportunity is what really counts. The exact grade you might make is not too important to you or to us. Naturally, however, we expect a somewhat high percentage of correct answers from you.

Answer as many questions as you can without referring to the previous lessons you have studied. If you find any difficult questions, then refer to the lessons. We expect you to do so!

Notice that these questions are divided into four parts—corresponding to the four lessons. We advise you not to cover more than one lesson at a sitting. Take sufficient time to understand each question.

Here are two EXAMPLES TO *SHOW YOU HOW* to answer the questions:

Read the *first question* of this test. The right answer to select, of course, is **"C."** Here is the second example: Notice question number **2** on the next page. The correct answer is **"B."** That is all there is to it! It is very simple and fast.

The procedure is always the same. Now continue with question **3** in the same manner...

LESSON 13: WHAT IS THE CHRISTIAN'S INHERITANCE?

1. To retain material studied with these lessons, it is best to:
   A. depend entirely on the memory, because taking notes is a waste of time.
   B. just READ the scripture references given in answer to lesson questions.
   C. WRITE DOWN the answers and conclusions so that they can be rapidly reviewed.
   D. write down the answers only, without adding any pertinent ideas of your own.

2. We can have positive assurance of what will happen to us after death because:
   A. this world's ministers tell us the facts.
   B. the Bible reveals it.
   C. our parents have taught us this knowledge.
   D. we can discover this vital information for ourselves.

3. Why is Abraham of important to Christians?
   A. Because of the promise God made to him.
   B. He isn't. He's just an Old Testament character of no significance.
   C. Only because God liked him.
   D. Certainly not because he is the 'father of the faithful'.

4. Was heaven promised to Abraham as a reward for righteousness?
   A. Yes, the Bible says so.
   B. We can't be sure.
   C. Only time will tell.
   D. Absolutely not!

5. Has any man, aside from Christ, ever ascended into heaven where God is?
   A. Yes, all the 'good' people who have ever lived.
   B. Who can tell, for the Bible does not say.
   C. No one but Christ has ascended to heaven.
   D. Yes, all those who had rigidly made up their minds, before they died, that they were going there.

6. Is this earth basically such an undesirable place that one could NEVER desire it as an eternal inheritance?
   A. Yes.
   B. No, for it is a desirable inheritance just as it is.
   C. No, for it would be a very desirable inheritance if sin and the results of sin were removed from it.
   D. The earth could NEVER be a desirable inheritance under any conditions.

7. Did Abraham have to be obedient before God's promise was made certain to him?
   A. He certainly did!
   B. It would be unfair of God, the Creator and Sustainer, to ask that of anyone.
   C. Bible records do not reveal this.
   D. Obedience had nothing to do with God's promise to Abraham.

8. Was Abraham actually promised the EARTH forever?
   A. The Bible is not specific about this.
   B. Yes, the Bible clearly shows that God's original promise to Abraham EXPANDED until it includes eternal inheritance of the whole earth.
   C. No, he was promised heaven.
   D. We are promised the earth forever, but Abraham wasn't.

9. Since the Christian is promised ETERNAL inheritance of the earth, does this also mean that one must have eternal life in order to receive one's inheritance?
   A. Yes, for ETERNAL inheritance obviously involves and includes everlasting life.
   B. Not necessarily.
   C. It would seem so, but it really isn't true.
   D. Definitely not!

10. Was the promise of everlasting inheritance made to anyone else besides Abraham?
    A. No.
    B. Yes, to a 'Seed'.
    C. The Bible says the promise was made to Abraham ONLY!
    D. The Bible is vague on this point.

11. The word 'Seed' in Genesis 3:15 refers to:
    A. Christ.
    B. the Jews.

   C. a kind of garden seed.
   D. an offspring of one of the Gentile nations.

12. What territory did God ORIGINALLY promise to Abraham?
    A. An area in Russia.
    B. An area in South America.
    C. The area of often called Palestine.
    D. An area in heaven.

13. God promised to make Abraham:
    A. A seat at His right hand.
    B. A gatekeeper.
    C. A great nation.
    D. Head of security.

14. Was part of why Jesus died to allow Christians to have eternal inheritance?
    A. Of course not.
    B. Yes, the Bible says it does.
    C. It couldn't possibly include that.
    D. That would be too good to be true.

15. Does ETERNAL inheritance include EVERLASTING life?
    A. It wouldn't seem reasonable to think so.
    B. Obviously it does.
    C. Definitely not!
    D. That would depend upon one's OWN interpretation of the Bible.

16. In what manner do Abraham's modern-day, blood-descendants – the Israelites, which include the Jews – come in on the promise of eternal inheritance?
    A. Through the 'Seed' – Christ – by becoming a Christian.
    B. Through denying that Christ is the Savior.
    C. Through believing that Christ was just a good man, but nothing more.
    D. Through refusing to recognize Christ as their coming Ruler.

17. Through whom do GENTILE nations of today come in on the promise of eternal inheritance?
    A. They come in through a way other than that through which Abraham's blood-descendants come into the promise.
    B. They come in the same way as do Abraham's descendants – through Christ.
    C. They cannot come in on the promise.
    D. The Bible does not reveal this.

18. Do we also, like Abraham, have to be obedient to inherit the promise?
    A. No, for we are now under grace (cf. Ephesians 2:8-10).
    B. Absolutely not! – for the law has been done away.
    C. Of course not, for 'everyone knows that no one can keep the law', so no one can be obedient.
    D. Yes, the Bible shows we do (cf. Hebrews 5:9; Acts 5:32).

19. Does something have to happen to our mortal bodies before we can inherit the Kingdom of God?
    A. We are not told anything about this in the Bible.
    B. Yes, our mortal bodies must be changed into SPIRIT, for "flesh and blood cannot inherit the Kingdom of God."
    C. No change is necessary since our 'immortal souls' go to heaven when we die.
    D. Our mortal bodies need not be changed into spirit to inherit God's Kingdom.

20. When Jesus returns, will it take God a long time to change our bodies from mortal flesh to immortal spirit?
    A. Yes, for it is a difficult process.
    B. No, it will take but a 'moment'.
    C. Since our bodies are flesh and blood, it would naturally take considerable time to change them.
    D. Yes, for God does not perform miracles any more.

21. Which ONE of these four statements is RIGHT in respect to the true Christian?
    A. He cannot ever receive the promise made to Abraham.
    B. He does not have to be transformed – changed into spirit – to receive his promised inheritance.
    C. When changed to a spirit being he will not receive the same inheritance promised to Abraham.

D. When changed to a spirit being he will receive the same inheritance promised to Abraham.

22. Has Abraham received 'the promises' (Hebrews 11)?
    A. Yes, he received all the land.
    B. Hebrews 11 does not say.
    C. No.
    D. He is in heaven, so yes.

23. Abraham, the man God called out of the ways of this world and to whom He gave the promise of eternal inheritance,
    A. believed and obeyed God.
    B. demanded many signs and wonders before he would take any steps.
    C. was too much in love with the ways of this world to really want to make a change.
    D. could not make up his mind about following God's instructions.

LESSON 14: ARE HUMANS IMMORTAL?

24. The doctrine of the immortality of the soul arose from:
    A. the teachings of pagans and originated with Satan.
    B. the teachings of the Old Testament.
    C. the writings of the apostle Paul.
    D. the Protestant reformers who were the first to teach such a doctrine.

25. God formed Adam at creation:
    A. out of spirit.
    B. out of the dust of the ground.
    C. as an immortal spiritual soul encased in a material body.
    D. out of incorruptible and immortal flesh.

26. Humans are:
    A. not subject to death.
    B. immortal souls that continue to live on after death.
    C. living souls subject to death just like the beasts of the field.
    D. not like an animal in the sense that they does not die as do animals.

27. In the second century A.D., Justin (Martyr) taught:
    A. There is no resurrection.
    B. To follow Marcion of Pontus.
    C. That the prophetic word indicates that there were three Lords in number.
    D. Those who teach that when their souls die that they are taken to heaven are not Christians.

28. Which ONE of these four statements is FALSE?
    A. To give the first man life, God breathed air into him.
    B. The life of the flesh is the blood.
    C. The soul that sins will die.
    D. In addition to breathing air into the first man's nostrils, God placed within him an 'immortal soul'.

29. Eternal life:
    A. is the gift of God, who has eternal life inherent in Himself.
    B. is inherent in all humans from birth.
    C. is always given to people immediately upon their 'confessing Christ'.
    D. is a fable held by those who are 'religious'.

30. The ancient pagan Greek philosophers
    A. believed life always ended at death.
    B. did not have any influence on the Catholic Church.
    C. quoted from the Bible as their authority.
    D. used human reason to prove that man must have an immortal soul.

31. Physical science:
    A. can prove the existence of immortal souls.
    B. can disprove the existence of immortal souls.
    C. has no tools whereby it can determine or deny the existence of spiritual things.
    D. reveals all the laws concerning the spiritual world.

32. Science has proved:
    A. that physically, life comes from life.
    B. that the soul leaves the body at death.
    C. that there can be no resurrection.
    D. that man was not created, but rather evolved from warm ocean slime.

33. Which ONE of these four statements is TRUE? The

famous poet, Dante Alighieri, popularized
   A. scientific thinking.
   B. the law of biogenesis.
   C. Luther's teachings.
   D. the pagan concepts of paradise, purgatory and a non-detroying inferno.

34. Which ONE of these four statements is true?
    A. Humans continue to think even after they die.
    B. The Bible reveals nothing about the source of human life.
    C. God cannot destroy the wicked because they have immortal souls.
    D. The soul can die.

35. Which ONE of these four statements is FALSE?
    A. The word 'spirit' in the Bible sometimes refers to the mind of man.
    B. The word 'spirit' may also refer to God or an angel because God and angels are composed of spirit.
    C. The word 'spirit', when referring to an attribute of humans, may mean the breath.
    D. Whenever the word 'spirit' is used in regard to humans it means an 'immortal soul'.

36. Are animals and humans both souls?
    A. Yes, the Bible calls both humans and animals 'souls'.
    B. We cannot know because we can never be sure of what the Bible means.
    C. No, because souls cannot die, but animals can die.
    D. No, the Bible never calls an animal a 'soul'.

37. Which ONE of these four statements is FALSE?
    A. The Hebrew word NEPHESH, often translated 'soul', is also translated 'creature' when referring to animals.
    B. A human's mind is sometimes called a spirit because the functions of the human mind are made possible by the 'spirit in man'.
    C. The word 'spirit' is often translated from Hebrew or Greek words meaning 'breath' or 'wind' or 'air'.
    D. There is no need of a resurrection because man is already an 'immortal soul'.

38. Which ONE of these four statements is FALSE? In the Holy Bible:
    A. the word SOUL sometimes refers to the whole human.
    B. the word SOUL sometimes refers to the physical life of humans which is in the blood.
    C. the word SOUL sometimes refers to a dead body.
    D. the word SOUL means an 'immortal soul' inside of humans.

39. Both men and animals:
    A. were created to be equal.
    B. are breathing, mortal souls.
    C. have immortal souls residing in them that continue to think after death.
    D. have the hope of a resurrection.

40. What is death?
    A. The cessation of life.
    B. The portal through which humans pass into heaven or eternal punishing.
    C. The moment when the 'immortal soul' of a human, separated from the body for the first time, has an independent, conscious existence in another world.
    D. It is a human's best friend.

41. The Council of Lateran in 1513 decreed that:
    A. the soul is immortal and that all who deny this teaching are heretics and worthy of death.
    B. the Bible is the only source by which we can determine the nature of man.
    C. the soul is by nature mortal.
    D. all have a legitimate right to their own beliefs.

42. The subject of death should:
    A. not be studied because it is so 'mysterious'.
    B. be studied from the viewpoint of human reason.
    C. be studied by comparing the various philosophies of the world with one another for the answer.
    D. be studied by letting the Bible reveal just what death really is.

43. When a person dies, his/her thoughts:
    A. perish.
    B. thereafter are centered on the glory of God in heaven.

C. are at once devoted to the constant praise of God in heaven.
D. center about his/her past life in the flesh.

44. The fourth century Emperor Constantine:
    A. was a converted Christian.
    B. strove to combine sun-god worship practices into Christianity.
    C. was opposed to the use of idols.
    D. was a strong pacifist.

45. Which of the following was an original Christian view?
    A. The unsaved go to a place of suffering until the judgment.
    B. The resurrection of the body.
    C. Humans are reincarnated into some form of animal to live again on the earth after death.
    D. God intended that most would need to suffer eternity in the flames of Gehenna.

LESSON 15

46. Which ONE of these four statements is TRUE? The predominant view of people of the WORLD who believe in it, believe 'hell' to be a place:
    A. where a merciful God quickly causes the wicked to cease to exist.
    B. where God shows His love and mercy.
    C. which has not yet come into existence.
    D. where a vengeful God punishes the sinful forever with inconceivable torments.

47. IS there any such thing as a 'hell' mentioned in the Bible?
    A. No, the idea is a complete falsehood based only on man's imaginings.
    B. Of course not! A loving God would never allow any type of 'hell' to exist.
    C. There might be, but there is no way to know.
    D. Yes, for Christ speaks of Gehenna fire which is sometimes translated as 'hell'.

48. From where has the world received its FALSE concept of 'hell'?
    A. From God.
    B. From the pagans, who passed the idea to the 'Western religious leaders', who then taught it to others in the world.
    C. The world didn't receive it from anyone, for each person has thought out his own concept of eternal torment.
    D. It clearly came from Pacific Islanders who knew Jesus.

49. Would a just and loving God condemn to 'Gehenna fire' the vast majority of all the people who ever lived and never even heard about CHRISTIAN salvation – of SAVING KNOWLEDGE?
    A. Of course He would!
    B. Absolutely NOT!
    C. Perhaps.
    D. It is reasonable to believe He would.

50. Looking at the Greek, Christ talked about a 'Gehenna fire' in which one of the following scriptures?
    A. John 1:1.
    B. Hebrews 5:2.
    C. Mark 9:45.
    D. Mark 10:7.

51. The original Greek word 'hades' means:
    A. eternal torment.
    B. purgatory.
    C. the grave.
    D. paradise.

52. Gehenna fire:
    A. refers to the fire that burned in the 'Valley of Hinnom', which is a TYPE of the final 'lake of fire' that will consume all the incorrigible wicked.
    B. refers to the grave where people are buried.
    C. has no reference to either fire or the grave.
    D. refers to a reward for doing good deeds.

53. Which ONE of these four statements is TRUE about the fate of the incorrigibly wicked?
    A. God will not punish them.
    B. They will be given salvation without repentance or accepting Jesus as Savior.
    C. They will burn forever, but never be burnt up.
    D. They will be burnt up and essentially become ashes.

54. The 'lake of fire' will:
    A. not burn up the Beast and the False Prophet.
    B. be extinguished before any person can be put into it.
    C. have unrepentant sinners tossed into it.
    D. has no association with brimstone (sulphur).

55. The Bible's 'second death' occurs when:
    A. Jesus first returns.
    B. those guilty of persistent disobedience are tossed into the lake of fire.
    C. anyone who has been resurrected experiences another death.
    D. someone who has a 'near death experience' dies later.

56. When a person dies he or she:
    A. immediately goes to heaven, if he or she has led a 'good' life.
    B. immediately goes to fiery torment, if he or she has led a 'bad' life.
    C. ceases to exist until a resurrection, regardless of the kind of life he or she led.
    D. immediately goes to purgatory.

57. Which ONE of these four statements is TRUE? Most people:
    A. receive final judgment the moment they die.
    B. had it already, at birth, predestined to be saved or lost – they don't need any final judgment.
    C. will never be judged by God.
    D. receive final judgment after they are resurrected.

58. God says that all people will be judged by:
    A. His Word – the Holy Bible – which defines what sin is.
    B. whether or not they played cards to entertain themselves.
    C. whether or not they went to theaters.
    D. how many Christmas baskets they helped to distribute.

59. Your Bible says the 'wages of sin is':
    A. living eternally in outer darkness apart from God.
    B. eternal torment in the lake of fire.
    C. being destroyed forever by a worldwide flood.
    D. eternal death/destruction by fire.

60. The 'lake of fire' will:
    A. have no effect on the bodies of the wicked.
    B. only char the bodies of unrepentant people.
    C. be just hot enough to torment the wicked, but not burn them.
    D. utterly consume the wicked so they will cease existence.

61. The 'lake of fire' will result in:
    A. EVERLASTING fire burning in the cavernous depths of the earth.
    B. God putting it out before all the incorrigible wicked are burned up.
    C. this earth's surface burning up.
    D. being a place where the Devil torments the wicked for all eternity.

62. Which ONE of these four statements is TRUE?
    A. The earth's surface will only partially burn up when the wicked are destroyed.
    B. God promised to never destroy this earth's surface by fire.
    C. The entire earth's surface will burn when the unrepentant and man's works are consumed.
    D. Nowhere in the Bible does it say that the earth will burn.

63. The kindest thing God could do is
    A. to give rebellious, disobedient people ETERNAL LIFE so they can eternally continue tormenting themselves and others by their ways of sin.
    B. let this world continue forever in the way it is now going.
    C. to blot out all humankind when Jesus Christ returns.
    D. to destroy forever the life of anyone who REFUSES to live His better way of life.

64. The parable of Lazarus and the rich man proves:
    A. there is to be eternal punishing of the wicked.
    B. there is to be no punishment of the wicked.
    C. a 'lake of fire' will not exist.
    D. there is to be a resurrection of the righteous to eternal life.

LESSON 16
WHAT IT MEANS TO BE 'BORN AGAIN'!

65. Eternal life is:
    A. something you were born with.
    B. given only to those who regularly go to a priest and give their confession.
    C. given to all children at the time they are sprinkled in church.
    D. a free GIFT of God unmerited by human righteousness.

66. To 'be born again' means:
    A. to be baptized.
    B. to repent of sin.
    C. to accept Christ.
    D. to be changed into spirit at the resurrection — to be literally born into the Family of God!

67. In the resurrection true Christians shall:
    A. be made spirit and be born as the very Sons of God.
    B. be as we are now – only we shall live forever.
    C. basically become angels.
    D. not be like Christ.

68. God will give Christians eternal life:
    A. when we are BORN AGAIN at the resurrection.
    B. if they practice lawlessness.
    C. by creating immortal souls in us.
    D. without changing our mortal bodies.

69. When we are born again,
    A. we shall still be composed of flesh and blood.
    B. we shall be composed of spirit.
    C. we become members of the church.
    D. we can still sin.

70. Which ONE of these four statements is TRUE?
    A. We cannot sin when we are born of God.
    B. We are immediately born again when we 'confess Christ'.
    C. We are born again when we join the church of our choice.
    D. Our change from mortality to immortality does not take place at the resurrection.

71. The new birth involves:
    A. a complete change in the nature and composition of humans.
    B. swearing off movies, drink, and such.
    C. preaching Christ on street comers.
    D. doing what you think is right from henceforth.

72. We need the Holy Spirit of God:
    A. because that is the only way we can 'speak in tongues'.
    B. because that is the only way we can 'fall under the power'.
    C. because the Holy Spirit makes us immediately born again.
    D. because humans, born of physical parents, have no eternal life, and must receive the Holy Spirit which alone can impart it.

73. The Holy Spirit:
    A. is used as the impregnating 'germ' of eternal life.
    B. does not come from God the Father.
    C. is not promised to Christians.
    D. always comes with 'pentecostal manifestations'.

74. The conditions to receiving the Holy Spirit are:
    A. repent, believe and be baptized.
    B. waiting in a 'tarry meeting' and seeking to speak in tongues.
    C. do not include obedience to God.
    D. joining a church and taking the Lord's Supper every Sunday morning.

75. God gives the Holy Spirit ONLY to those who:
    A. perform miracles.
    B. disobey Him.
    C. obey Him.
    D. follow their conscience and do what society thinks is right.

76. Repentance, one of the conditions to receiving the Holy Spirit, means:
    A. doing penance.
    B. confessing Christ before men.
    C. doing what the church of your choice teaches.
    D. admitting your ways are wrong, asking God to forgive you, and changing to begin a new life of obedience to God and His laws.

77. You can know the difference between the HOLY

SPIRIT and any COUNTERFEIT spirit by:
A. whether or not one speaks in tongues.
B. whether or not one prophesies.
C. the fruits – such as, whether one is obedient or disobedient to the commandments of God.
D. no known means – we just have to accept each spirit as it comes along!

78. The fruits of the Spirit of God are:
A. singing and dancing and shouting 'in the spirit'!
B. love, joy, peace, patience, etc.
C. idolatry, failing to tithe, sabbath-breaking, etc.
D. joining a church and helping to make this a better world through worldly organizations.

79. When a human being receives the Holy Spirit, he or she:
A. feels the Spirit.
B. hears the Spirit.
C. cannot have the emotional experience of joy and happiness.
D. is begotten of God the Father.

80. Are Christians now only begotten, or are they already 'born' of God?
A. Neither. God cannot reproduce children.
B. Christians are now already born of God.
C. Christians are now already both begotten and born again. There is no difference.
D. They are not yet born of God. True Christians are now only the begotten children of God, awaiting the resurrection when they shall be born again, this time of spirit.

81. According to the Bible,
A. anyone who is now begotten of God cannot sin.
B. those who have received the Holy Spirit now are absolutely perfect.
C. we can have the mind of God if we receive the Holy Spirit.
D. spirit is not eternal.

Now That You've Finished …

FINAL INSTRUCTIONS

Keep this question section. File it in your notebook at the end of the Lessons it covers. Review these questions now and then. Why? Because the review will give you the opportunity to impress the true answers more firmly upon your mind.

Also, a review of the three false answers, given here for each question will aid you to realize more clearly some of the false ideas which you may have taken for granted. You will thereby grasp and retain the truth much better when it is presented to you.

ANSWERS TO TEST 4:

1-C	10-B	19-B	28-D	37-D	46-D	55-B	64-D	73-A
2-B	11-A	20-B	29-A	38-D	47-D	56-C	65-D	74-A
3-A	12-C	21-D	30-D	39-B	48-B	57-D	66-D	75-C
4-D	13-C	22-C	31-C	40-A	49-B	58-A	67-A	76-D
5-C	14-B	23-A	32-A	41-A	50-C	59-D	68-A	77-C
6-C	15-B	24-A	33-D	42-D	51-C	60-D	69-B	78-B
7-A	16-A	25-B	34-D	43-A	52-A	61-C	70-A	79-D
8-B	17-B	26-C	35-D	44-B	53-D	62-C	71-A	80-D
9-A	18-D	27-D	36-A	45-B	54-C	63-D	72-D	81-C

Grade Yourself:

Simply count the number of questions you missed. Your grade percentage will be next to that number below:

1-99	5-94	9-89	13-84	17-78	21-73
2-97	6-92	10-87	14-82	18-77	22-72
3-96	7-91	11-86	15-81	19-76	23-71
4-95	8-90	12-85	16-80	20-75	24-70

Faith for Those God has Called and Chosen

Do you know much about faith? Do you know how important faith is?

Jesus said, that along with mercy and judgment, faith was one of the weightier, more important, matters of the law (Matthew 23:23). His disciples realized that faith was important.

One day:

> 5 ...the apostles said to the Lord, "Increase our faith" (Luke 17:5, NKJV except where indicated elsewhere: though the What is Faith? booklet, quotes from the KJV, without separate notice).

Instead of actually telling them how to increase their faith, Jesus suggested that they had only a little.

But in other parts of the Bible, Jesus and others gave more details about how faith could be increased. This short booklet will discuss several, but not all, aspects of faith. The NKJV of the Bible, for example, has the English word 'faith' 243 times in the New Testament (twice in the Old) and the word faithful 53 times in the NT (and 32 in the OT).

Show Faith By Doing, Not Just Claiming to Believe

Paul wrote:

> 7 "For we walk by faith, not by sight" (2 Corinthians 5:7).

In practical terms, this means that we live God's way of life even when we have trials and temptations, when things seem almost hopeless, or when others try to deceive us. Paul also wrote:

> 31 "Do we then make void the law through faith? Certainly not! On the contrary, we establish the law" (Romans 3:31).

Furthermore, James wrote:

> 17 Thus also faith by itself, if it does not have works, is dead. 18 But someone will say, "You have faith, and I have works." Show me your faith without your works, and I will show you my faith by my works. 19 You believe that there is one God. You do well. Even the demons believe - and tremble! 20 But do you want to know, O foolish man, that faith without works is dead? 21 Was not Abraham our father justified by works when he offered Isaac his son on the altar? 22 Do you see that faith was working together with his works, and by works faith was made perfect? (James 2:17-22).

Thus faith goes beyond just believing.

Living faith includes action that God approves - living as Jesus did and as He wanted His followers to do. Not only keeping the Sabbath or God's Holy Days when it seems difficult, but to tithe, avoid pagan holidays like Christmas, and to be honest in a dishonest society. Also, to love those who do not love you (Matthew 5:44-48). Abraham's faith was shown by obedience in works and how he lived his life, not in the manifestation of miracles from his prayers. Abraham had living faith. It takes faith to live God's way in this world.

Jesus taught:

> 48 Therefore you shall be perfect, just as your Father in heaven is perfect. (Matthew 5:48)

We are not saved by works, but by faith:

> 8 For by grace you have been saved through

faith, and that not of yourselves; it is the gift of God, 9 not of works, lest anyone should boast. 10 For we are His workmanship, created in Christ Jesus for good works, which God prepared beforehand that we should walk in them. (Ephesians 2:8-10)

Notice the Bible shows that although we are saved by grace, even that is the gift of God. Also notice that we were created in Christ Jesus for good works.

What is the Bible Definition of Faith?

The Bible gives a definition of faith:

> 1 Now faith is the foundation of things hoped for, the evidence of things not seen. 2 For by it the elders obtained a good testimony. 3 By faith we understand that the worlds were framed by the word of God, so that the things which are seen were not made of things which are visible...6 But without faith it is impossible to please Him, for he who comes to God must believe that He is, and that He is a rewarder of those who diligently seek Him " (Hebrews 11:1-3,6, modified NKJV).

Author's Note: The preceding was modified as the KJV and NKJV translate the Greek word hypostasis as substance but it literally means under (hypo) stability (stasis) or foundation. Hence, faith is the underlying stability that God's people are to have.

Do you really believe that God is rewarding those He has called and chosen, those who seek Him? If so, how does that affect your life?

The Greek word most commonly translated in the New Testament as faith is πίστις, which is transliterated into English as pistis. BibleSoft defines it to mean:

> πίστις pistis (pis'- tis) persuasion, i.e. credence; moral conviction (of religious truth, or the truthfulness of God or a religious teacher), especially reliance upon Christ for salvation; abstractly, constancy in such profession; by extension, the system of religious (Gospel) truth itself: (Biblesoft's New Exhaustive Strong's Numbers and Concordance with Expanded Greek-Hebrew Dictionary. Copyright © 1994, 2003, 2006 Biblesoft, Inc. and International Bible Translators, Inc.)

By system of truth, at least one minister felt that it included the concept of the work, and since Christians are part of the work of God, it is fair to say that faith is part of the work. And it certainly does take significant faith at times to do the work. Notice something that Christians are told to do:

> 3...contend earnestly for the faith which was once for all delivered to the saints. (Jude 3)

Jude is writing to Christians, those who have been called and chosen (1 Corinthians 1:26-28; Matthew 22:14). We are not just to have faith, but promote it (Matthew 24:14; 28:19-20). That is what we in the Continuing Church of God are striving to do.

The Called and Chosen are to be Faithful

While close to all truly in the churches of Christ (Romans 16:16b) believe that they have been called and chosen, all should realize that they are also to be faithful.

When Jesus returns, notice who is with Him:

> 14... He is Lord of lords and King of kings; and those who are with Him are called, chosen, and faithful. (Revelation 17:14)

We who are called and chosen need to remain faithful. We are not just to obey God, we need to have faith that His ways are best for us.

Notice two other passages of scripture:

> 18 For I consider that the sufferings of this present time are not worthy to be compared with the glory which shall be revealed in us. 19 For the earnest expectation of the creation eagerly waits for the revealing of the sons of God. (Romans 8:18-19)

28 And we know that all things work together for good to those who love God, to those who are the called according to His purpose. (Romans 8:28)

When things go wrong, we need faith to endure to the end. It sometimes takes faith to realize that all things work together for our good.

Faith vs. Feeling

Many confuse feelings with faith. While the faithful should have a godly confidence, faith is not really an emotion to be temporarily worked up.

Now, it is true if Satan is bothering one, immediate action should be taken:

> 7 Therefore submit to God. Resist the devil and he will flee from you. 8 Draw near to God and He will draw near to you. Cleanse your hands, you sinners; and purify your hearts, you double-minded. (James 4:7-8)

> 5..."God resists the proud, But gives grace to the humble." 6 Therefore humble yourselves under the mighty hand of God, that He may exalt you in due time, 7 casting all your care upon Him, for He cares for you. 8 Be sober, be vigilant; because your adversary the devil walks about like a roaring lion, seeking whom he may devour. 9 Resist him, steadfast in the faith, knowing that the same sufferings are experienced by your brotherhood in the world. 10 But may the God of all grace, who called us to His eternal glory by Christ Jesus, after you have suffered a while, perfect, establish, strengthen, and settle you. (1 Peter 5:5-10)

And taking those biblical actions should increase faith.

But that is not the same as some type of emotional session to temporarily make someone feel that they have faith.

In his What is Faith booklet the late Church of God leader Herbert Armstrong wrote:

WHY People Lack Faith

And now, very briefly, WHY don't we have FAITH, and how may we get it, and how may it be increased? So many say, "Well, I have no impression -- I have no feeling, no conviction -- that I shall get the answer."

They want to wait until they get a certain CONVICTION, a certain FEELING, a sort of assurance they can FEEL - before they really believe they shall have the answer.

But THAT is not faith!

That is FEELING!

Your feeling, your convictions, your impressions, has absolutely not one thing or the other to do with FAITH. FAITH HAS ONLY TO DO WITH GOD'S WORD! The one question is, Has God promised it in the Bible? If He has, then probabilities, possibilities, feelings, convictions, impressions, have nothing whatsoever to do with it. God has a thousand ways we know nothing of, of answering and providing whatever He has promised. We don't need to see HOW He is going to do it.

And that's another thing - He almost never will do it the WAY we expect. So don't try to figure out how it is possible for God to do it. You are trusting in SUPER-NATURAL POWER! Then BELIEVE in that power. God works in mysterious ways His wonders to perform. What He has promised, He will perform; but He will do it HIS way, and in HIS TIME. Leave all that to HIM and just TRUST HIM. Rely upon His word.

God's GIFT

And let us remember, FAITH is the GIFT OF GOD. So many think that everything else that comes from God is His gift, but the FAITH required to receive these things is something we ourselves must somehow work up, or strain and strive for. But we have to just relax and TRUST GOD, even for the FAITH by which we receive everything else! (Eph. 2:8).

In Revelation 14:12 is a description of the true Church of THIS DAY. Those in this Church have the FAITH OF JESUS. Notice, the FAITH OF JESUS! It is not just our faith in HIM, but His faith-- the very faith with which He performed His miracles--placed in us and acting in us. How can you get it? Draw closer to God. Get to know God. Surrender all the way to HIM, and do His will. And then PRAY. YOU get to know Him in PRAYER. We are too close to the material things. Through PRAYER, much more prayer, you can come closer to GOD and the spiritual things. And what a happy, joyous experience it is, once you have really done it!

Faith is the gift of God (Ephesians 2:8), but it is a gift that Christians can develop. Not through emotional appeals, but through living as Jesus lived and trusting God to see us through tests and trials. Feelings can be deceptive, faith is true.

The Just Shall Live By Faith

Christians are chosen to become rich in faith:

> 5 Listen, my beloved brethren: Has God not chosen the poor of this world to be rich in faith and heirs of the kingdom which He promised to those who love Him? (James 2:5)

The Bible, in three places teaches the just shall live by faith.

The first time is Habakkuk 2:4:

> 4 Behold the proud, His soul is not upright in him; But the just shall live by his faith.

The contrast between the proud and the just indicates that the faithful are not among the proud, but among the upright. The proud have too much faith in themselves.

Paul wrote:

> 11 But that no one is justified by the law in the sight of God is evident, for "the just shall live by faith." 12 Yet the law is not of faith, but "the man who does them shall live by them." (Galatians 3:11-12)

This last verse shows that while the law is not faith, the faithful will keep it.

In Romans 1:17-19, the Apostle Paul wrote:

> 17 For in it the righteousness of God is revealed from faith to faith; as it is written, "The just shall live by faith." 18 For the wrath of God is revealed from heaven against all ungodliness and unrighteousness of men, who suppress the truth in unrighteousness, 19 because what may be known of God is manifest in them, for God has shown it to them.

Regarding righteousness of God, Psalm 119:172 states:

> 172 My tongue shall speak of Your word, For all Your commandments are righteousness.

Hebrews says this about some of the just that were faithful:

> 13 These all died in faith, not having received the promises, but having seen them afar off were assured of them, embraced them and confessed that they were strangers and pilgrims on the earth. 14 For those who say such things declare plainly that they seek a homeland. 15 And truly if they had called to mind that country from which they had come out, they would have had opportunity to return. 16 But now they desire a better, that is, a heavenly country. Therefore God is not ashamed to be called their God, for He has prepared a city for them. (Hebrews 11:13-16)

So the faithful, while living God's way of life on Earth, are focused on the hope of their future reward with God. They "seek first the kingdom" (Matthew 6:33). But also on Earth they keep the commandments:

> 12 Here is the patience of the saints; here are those who keep the commandments of God and the faith of Jesus. (Revelation 14:12)

But it is not always easy to be part of the faithful. The expression 'patience of the saints' indicates great difficulty at that time. But with the faith OF Jesus, which God grants, we can endure. Sometimes we have to endure that which seems unfair (James:12-16) and/or for a very long period of time (2 Peter 3:8-9). Do not succumb to bitterness (cf. Hebrews 12:14-15; James 3:14).

Notice something the Apostle Paul wrote:

> 20 And I live, now not I; but Christ liveth in me. And that I live now in the flesh: I live in the faith of the Son of God, who loved me, and delivered himself for me. (Galatians 2:20, DRB)

We need to have the faith OF Jesus to have Him live His life in us. If this were not possible, the Bible would not teach that!

Recall that the Bible ties faith in with hope. Faith is the substance/foundation of things hoped for (Hebrews 11:1). Hope is something that we need to have:

> 15 And have hope toward God, which they themselves also allow, that there shall be a resurrection of the dead, both of the just and unjust. 16 And herein do I exercise myself, to have always a conscience void of offence toward God, and toward men. (Acts 24:15-16 KJV)

Not only is hope to be exercised, so essentially is faith. One exercises faith by living by it. And this is not simply a 'blind faith.' Notice that the Bible teaches:

> 21 Prove all things; hold fast that which is good. 22 Abstain from all appearance of evil. (1 Thessalonians 5:21-22 KJV)

The Bible teaches that one should be able to prove that there is a God:

> 20 For since the creation of the world His invisible attributes are clearly seen, being understood by the things that are made, even His eternal power and Godhead, so that they are without excuse, (Romans 1:20)

Of course, we must also look beyond the physical:

> 16 Therefore we do not lose heart. Even though our outward man is perishing, yet the inward man is being renewed day by day. 17 For our light affliction, which is but for a moment, is working for us a far more exceeding and eternal weight of glory, 18 while we do not look at the things which are seen, but at the things which are not seen. For the things which are seen are temporary, but the things which are not seen are eternal. (2 Corinthians 4:16-18)

By living according to faith, one also helps prove that the commands and instructions in the word of God are true - Christians do not simply have a blind, illogical, or emotional faith. Faith is real - it is the substance of things hoped for (Hebrews 11:1).

How Will God Judge You?

This article was originally published in December 1975 in the old Good News magazine by the old Worldwide Church of God and authored by the late Dennis Luker.

An ancient patriarch once asked God: "Shall not the Judge of all the earth do right?" Would you have had the courage (or the foolhardiness) to ask God such a seemingly presumptuous question?

The truth is that a very good friend of God's did, indeed, ask him that very question! And believe it or not, God wasn't at all upset with this righteous man. But my point is this: the Bible leaves no doubt that God is indeed the Judge of all human flesh (Ps. 75:7; Gen. 18:25; Ps. 96:13).

Christ Will Judge

One of the most basic biblical teachings is that Jesus Christ will return to this earth and establish the government of God to rule all nations. The prophet Isaiah wrote: "And he shall judge among the nations, and shall rebuke many people: and they shall beat their swords into plowshares, and their spears into pruninghooks: nation shall not lift up sword against nation, neither shall they learn war any more" (Isa. 2:4). This hasn't happened yet, but it is going to — and very possibly in our generation (see Matt. 24:3, 21-22, 30).

Isaiah's prophecy continues: "Behold, the day of the Lord cometh, cruel both with wrath and fierce anger, to lay the land desolate: and he shall destroy the sinners thereof out of it.... And I [God] will punish the world for their evil, and the wicked for their iniquity; and I will cause the arrogancy of the proud to cease, and will lay low the haughtiness of the terrible" (Isa. 13:9, 11). "The day of the Lord" refers to the time when Christ returns with fierce anger to rebuke the nations.

We are admonished: "Fear God, and give glory to him; for the hour of his judgment is come..." (Rev. 14:7). Why fear God? Because "God shall bring every work into judgment, with every secret thing, whether it be good, or whether it be evil" (Eccl. 12:14).

Isaiah also declares: "... For out of Zion shall go forth the law, and the word of the Lord from Jerusalem" (Isa. 2:3).

Righteous judgment takes into consideration the knowledge and understanding a person possesses. It is fair, just, impartial judgment — one standard for all — considering attitude, ability, and any number of other factors.

At Christ's return, the laws and principles of the Bible will be His guide for judgment — the standard of truth and righteousness (Ps. 119:142, 172; John 17:17).

How Christ Will Judge

Jesus Christ of Nazareth said: "Judge not according to the appearance, but judge righteous judgment" (John 7:24). What is "righteous judgment"? Samuel, who judged Israel, wrote: "... For the Lord seeth not as man seeth; for man looketh on the outward appearance, but the Lord looketh on the heart (I Sam. 16:7). Righteous judgment takes into consideration the knowledge and understanding a person possesses. It is fair, just, impartial judgment — one standard for all without respect of persons — considering attitude, ability, and any number of other factors.

The apostle Paul explained: "For there is no respect of persons with God. For as many as have sinned without law shall also perish without law: and as many as have sinned in the law shall be judged by the law" (Rom. 2:11-12). He is explaining here that those who know the law shall be judged by it when Christ returns. But, those that "have sinned without [knowledge of the] law shall also perish without [being judged by the] law." They will be resurrected to physical life later in God's plan, be given the knowledge of God's law and then "judged according to their works" (Rev. 20:12).

Is God Fair?

Even though all people will not have the knowledge of God's spiritual law at the time of Christ's return, they will still be dealt with "everyone after his ways" (Ezek. 33:20) — according to how they have lived by what they understood. "He will punish sin wherever it is found. He will punish the heathen when they sin, even though they never had God's written laws, for down in their hearts they know right from wrong" (Rom. 2:14-15, The Living Bible).

God is fair! When Christ returns, each person will be dealt with justly and honestly according to how he has lived. Jesus said: "And that servant, which knew his lord's will, and prepared not himself, neither did according to his will, shall be beaten with many stripes. But he that knew not, and did commit things worthy of stripes, shall be beaten with few stripes...." (Luke 12:47-48). So even those who have not yet been called to know the will of God when Christ returns shall be punished for the things they did wrong — but with fewer "stripes" than those who knew God's will and didn't do it. Christ will deal with all people according to what they know and understand and how they act upon it.

The New Testament emphasizes three main principles of judgment which Christ will use to judge those of us who know His will.

1) Judged According to Our Works

The first principle of judgment is that "we shall be judged according to our works." Peter wrote: "And if ye call on the Father, who without respect of persons judgeth according to every man's work, pass the time of your sojourning here in fear" (I Pet. 1:17). And Jesus said: "For the Son of man shall come in the glory of his Father with his angels; and then he shall reward every man according to his works" (Matt. 16:27). This is repeated many times in the New Testament (see Rom. 2:6; I Cor. 3:8; James 2:14; Rev. 2:23; 11:18; 20:12).

Our 'works' means our 'way of life' — our Christian overcoming, growing, serving — or lack of it. Our 'works' also includes our part in helping do the Work of God today{supporting Matthew 24:14; 28:19-20} ... doing the true Work of God on earth. It should be very motivating to realize that we shall be judged and rewarded according to how well we do in our Christian efforts!

However, we are not saved by even our good works (see Eph. 2:8-10; Titus 3:5).

Christ will judge each one of us according to what we accomplished with all we have been given. But if we don't grow at all, we will be rejected and our reward given to someone who did overcome and grow spiritually.

2) Judged According to Our Ability

The second principle of judgment is explained in the parable of the talents in Matthew 25 and Luke 19. Jesus explained: "For the kingdom of heaven is as a man travelling into a far country, who called his own servants, and delivered unto them his goods. And unto one he gave five talents, to another two, and to another one; to every man according to his several ability; and straightway took his journey. Then he that had received the five talents went and traded with the same, and made them other five talents. And likewise he that had received two, he also gained other two" (Matt. 25:14-17). The words 'traded with' in the original Greek language imply 'working with' or 'using'. Jesus continued: "After a long time the lord of those servants cometh, and reckoneth with them" (verse 19).

When Christ returns, He will call all of us to Him to find out how much we have grown or increased the 'talents' He has given us. To those who have used and increased their God-given abilities, He will say: "Well done, thou good and faithful servant: thou hast been faithful over a few things, I will make thee ruler over many things: enter thou into the joy of thy lord" (verse 21).

The servant who did not use or develop his one "talent" made excuses and said: " I was afraid, and went and hid your talent in the earth: 10, there thou hast that is thine" (verse 25). He knew Christ expected him to grow and bear fruit (verse 24), but he was lazy and didn't do it.

In Luke's account of this same parable, Jesus said: "Out of thine own mouth will I judge thee, thou wicked servant. Thou knewest that I was an austere man, taking up that I laid not down, and reaping that I did not sow.... And he said unto them that stood by, Take from him the pound, and give it to him that hath ten pounds.... For I say unto you, That unto every one which hath shall be given; and from him that hath not, even that he hath shall be taken away from him" (Luke 19:22,24,26).

So the second principle of judgment is: We shall be judged according to what we do with what we have been given. Christ will consider everything when He judges us — our heredity, environment, upbringing, educational opportunities, etc. Everyone is different. We all have different abilities and varying amounts of education. Some have inherited more 'talents' than others. Some have had better and more opportunities in life. This is why Christ said: "For unto whomsoever much is given, of him shall be much required..." (Luke 12:48).

Christ will judge each one of us according to what we have accomplished with all we have been given. But if we don't grow at all, we will be rejected and our reward given to someone who did overcome and grow spiritually (Matt. 25:29-30).

3) Judged As We Judge Others

In His Sermon on the Mount, Jesus taught: "Judge not, that ye be not judged. For with what judgment ye judge, ye shall be judged: and with what measure ye mete, it shall be measured to you again" (Matt. 7:1-2). In other words, 'You shall be judged as you judge others'.

James wrote: "So speak ye, and so do, as they that shall be judged by the law of liberty. For he shall have judgment without mercy, that hath shewed no mercy; and mercy rejoices against judgment" (James 2:12-13). If you are not merciful and forgiving toward others, God will not be merciful toward you in your day of judgment.

All of us need to remember these words of Jesus Christ: "If ye forgive men their trespasses, your heavenly Father will also forgive you: But if ye forgive not men their trespasses, neither will your Father forgive your trespasses" (Matt. 6:14-15). Do you want to be forgiven your sins and mistakes and be judged with mercy? Then overlook the faults and mistakes of others and be merciful, humble and forgiving in dealing with others.

Finally, remember Paul's inspired words to the Christians in Rome: "But why dost thou judge thy brother? or why dost thou set at nought thy brother? for we shall all stand before the judgment seat of Christ. For it is written, As I live, saith the Lord, every knee shall bow to me, and every tongue shall confess to God. So then every one of us shall give account of himself to God" (Rom. 14:10-12).

A Merciful God!

Especially as we are merciful to others, God Almighty and Jesus Christ will be merciful in judging us. Jesus promised in the Sermon on the Mount: "Blessed are the merciful: for they shall obtain mercy" (Matt. 5:7). God says: "For I am merciful" (Jer. 3:12). Anyone striving to do his Creator's will can count on the mercy of God.

Many patriarchs, prophets and kings in past ages have experienced the incredible, almost unbelievable mercy of their Maker. The Almighty God forgave Abraham of his foibles in the flesh; He forgave David, upon real repentance, of the capital sins of adultery and murder; He forgave even the wicked king Manasseh when he finally came to himself.

There is no sin bigger than the mercy of God, so long as the real desire to repent is present within the sinner. Read Psalm 136.

You can be sure that God, in judgment, will take everything possible into account on your behalf. Never take yourself out of the realm of His mercy. God will never leave you or forsake you. Guard against ever forsaking Him and His way of life.

Don't you want to hear the words: "Well done, thou good and faithful servant, enter thou into the joy of thy lord"?

How will God judge you?

Editor: Let me add that in these end times, the majority of Christians are Laodicean. Those remaining that way do not properly judge themselves (Revelation 3:14-20). Instead they tend to be judges (the Greek terms transliterated as lao & dicea basically mean "people judge"). Laodiceans consider something other than Matthew 6:33, 24:14 and 28:19-20 to be their priority. Sometimes it is wrong doctrinal priorities (cf. Titus 3:9-11) and/or fear to what they should (Matthew 25:25-29), while normally combined with a lukewarm attitude to the proper work of the church (Revelation 3:15-16).

More FREE *Continuing Church of God* Books and Booklets
at www.ccog.org/books

The Gospel of the Kingdom of God

Is God Calling You?

Is God's Existence Logical?

Prayer: What Does the Bible Teach?

Proof Jesus is the Messiah

The Decalogue, Christianity, and the Beast

Should You Keep God's Holy Days or Demonic Holidays?

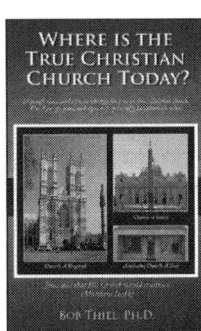
Where Is The True Christian Church Today?

Questions and Answers

Here are some questions and answers that some have wondered about.

Q. The Bible teaches that we are to honor our father and mother, but I have a problem. I do not know and have never known my father (or, for some their mothers). How can I honor him (or her)?

A. A lot of young people face the same type of situation you face. The basic thing to do is to honor the parent that you know and not worry too much about the one you do not. You can always pray for your other parent that he (or she) will be blessed by God). God does not expect you to do something totally out of your control.

The commandment in Deuteronomy is stated as follows:

16 'Honor your father and your mother, as the Lord your God has commanded you, that your days may be long, and that it may be well with you in the land which the Lord your God is giving you. (Deuteronomy 5:16)

Keeping this commandment helps show proper respect for authority, and will help you lead a better and fuller life.

Of course, God is our spiritual Father, and we are to honor Him, whether or not our human father is around.

Q: "Concerning makeup: Is it wrong for a woman to wear it?"

A: The Bible does not give a definite 'yea or nay' regarding the use of makeup. Some cite the negative example of Jezebel painting her face to support a 'no makeup' stand. But Jezebel was condemned for her wrong motivation and her evil actions rather than the use of makeup per se.

On the positive side, one of Job's beautiful daughters was named Kerenhappuch. Translated from the Hebrew this means 'horn of eye-paint' or 'horn of cosmetics'. The Jerusalem Bible translates her name 'Mascara'. Christ's and Paul's examples were to respect the outward physical customs of the day. Christ blended in with crowds because there was nothing striking or outlandishly different about His appearance.

I Peter 3:3,4 tells Christian women not to rely on elaborate hairdos, jewelry, or clothing for adornment, but rather on a beautiful heart or personality. But it is certainly right to look attractive. Ezekiel 16 speaks of God symbolically adorning His 'bride', Israel, with jewelry and silk.

Whether or not one wears makeup is a matter of personal preference. Some women prefer not to wear it at all. God wants us to 'dress and keep' our bodies and make the most of what He has given us. And makeup worn in moderation and good taste can be beneficial to a woman's appearance." (Q&A. Good News magazine, January 1976, p. 13)

I do not want to see God's women dressing and grooming so VERY plainly and UNworldly that they appear to be wearing a 'religious uniform'. That is, to set themselves so far off from 'the world' as a whole that they actually APPEAR 'religious' -- and, also, a little ridiculous. And frankly, some of our women DO - they go too far to the extreme in plainness. "Our women must avoid the overdone Hollywood glamour-girl grooming on the one hand, and the plain UN-beautiful eyesore 'religious uniform' appearance on the other. Both men and women should dress in a manner that does not attract special attention because of grooming or appearance too far from the average. And we should take a little pride in our appearance -- not from VANITY, but to be pleasing to others ... If, ... on make-up, some woman appears too far toward overdoing it, the minister should speak to her privately about it -- kindly -- but still admonishing her." (Armstrong, HW. Ministerial Bulletin, October 23, 1974)

It should be pointed out that in the Continuing Church of God (CCOG) we do NOT require that anyone wear makeup. Perhaps it should also be mentioned that Wayne Pyle, who was an employee of the old Worldwide Church of God (WCG), reported that Herbert W. Armstrong basically always wore makeup while filming the World Tomorrow program, even when WCG prohibited makeup (which it did at least 2 times). Bob Thiel does not wear makeup when in the CCOG videos as the lights are not so bright as to make that needful.

Q: In Exodus 13:4, the month Abib is mentioned. Does Abib mean our month of September? I am puzzled.

A: Abib (also called Nisan in Esther 3:7) is the first month of the Hebrew Calendar, corresponding to our March/April. In 2020, it begins after sunset on March 25th on the Roman calendar (the one most people use in the 21st century).

More information on the calendar can be found in the free booklet, online at www.ccog.org, titled Should You Keep God's Holy Days or Demonic Holidays?

Q: "I get the feeling from all I've read that to become a Christian is about the most difficult thing in the world, so difficult that I have great qualms as to whether I could ever qualify or 'make it' myself!"

A: Christ said that His yoke is easy and his burden light (Matt. II :29-30). All you have to do to become a Christian is to believe, repent of sin and be baptized (Acts 2:38; Mark 1:15). Repentance is the gift of God; it is not something you can work up for yourself (Rom. 2:4; II Tim. 2:25). If you truly want to change your life and live Christ's way, according to the law of love (James 2:8), then you have already been granted that gift. You should be baptized as soon as possible (Acts 8:36). ...

A person doesn't have to 'qualify' or be perfect to be baptized-he {or she} just has to want to live God's way.

A Christian is one who grows toward perfection (Matt. 5:48). The apostle Paul, years after he was baptized, said the following: "It seems to be a fact of life that when I want to do what is right, I inevitably do what is wrong.... In my mind I want to be God's willing servant but instead I find myself still enslaved to sin .... Oh, what a terrible predicament I'm in! Who will free me from my slavery to this deadly lower nature?" Paul then went on to say, "Thank God! It has been done by Jesus Christ our Lord. He has set me free" (Rom. 7:21-25, The Living Bible).

God loves you and wants you to be in His Kingdom. The very fact that you are reading this magazine is pretty good evidence you are being called now, and if God is calling you, then you can 'make it' into His Kingdom. Romans 8:30-32 reads: "Those whom he called he also justified; and those whom he justified he also glorified. What then shall we say to this? If God is for us, who is against us? He who did not spare his own Son but gave him up for us all, will he not also give us all things with him? (Q&A. Good News magazine, January 1976, p. 13).

Do not give on God (Matthew 10:22) and God will not give up on you! "He who has begun a good work in you will complete it until the day of Jesus" (Philippians 1:6).

For more information, check out our free booklets, available online at www.ccog.org, titled Christians: Ambassadors for the Kingdom of God, Biblical instructions on living as a Christian and Is God Calling You?

Made in the USA
Lexington, KY
13 December 2019